PIANO ★ VOCAL ★ GUITAR

FREEDOM RK

ISBN 978-1-5400-0395-9

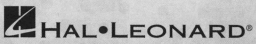

HAL•LEONARD®

7777 W. BLUEMOUND RD. P.O. BOX 13819 MILWAUKEE, WI 53213

Visit Hal Leonard Online at
www.halleonard.com

ABRAHAM, MARTIN AND JOHN

Words and Music by
RICHARD HOLLER

peo - ple, but it seems the good die young. __ But I just looked a -

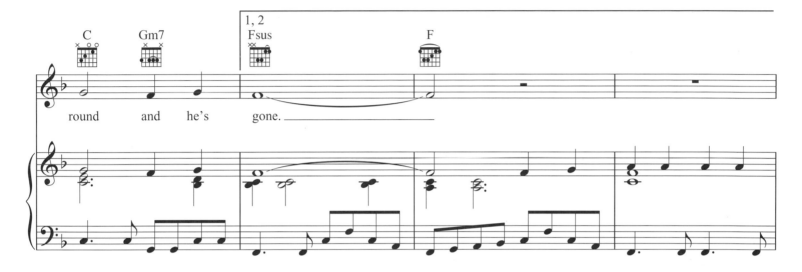

round and he's gone. _____

Has gone. _____

Did - n't you love __ the things they __

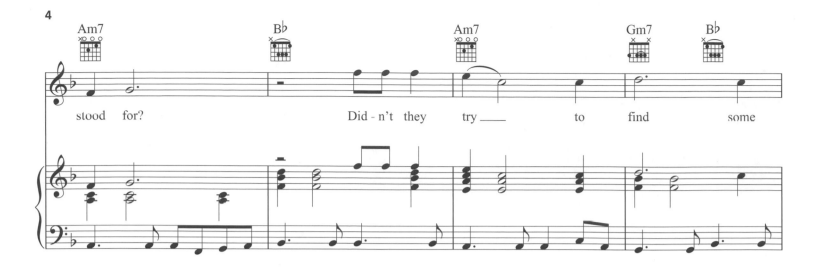

stood for?   Did - n't they   try _____ to find some

good   for   you and me?   And

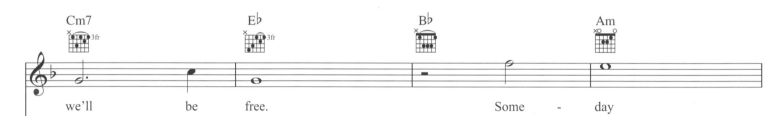

we'll   be   free.   Some - day

soon   it's gon - na be _ one day. Has an - y - bod - y here seen my

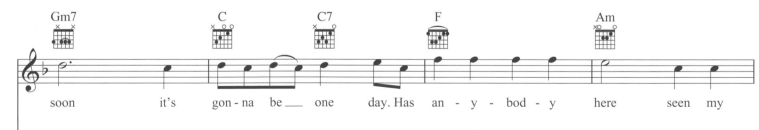

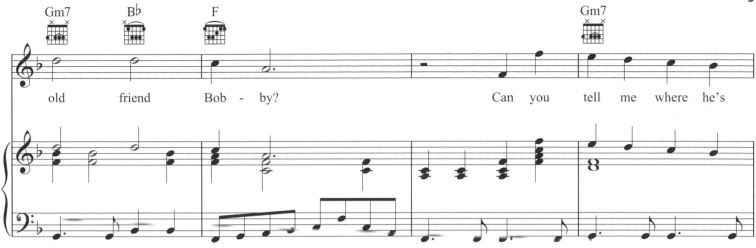

BLACK AND WHITE

Words by DAVID ARKIN
Music by EARL ROBINSON

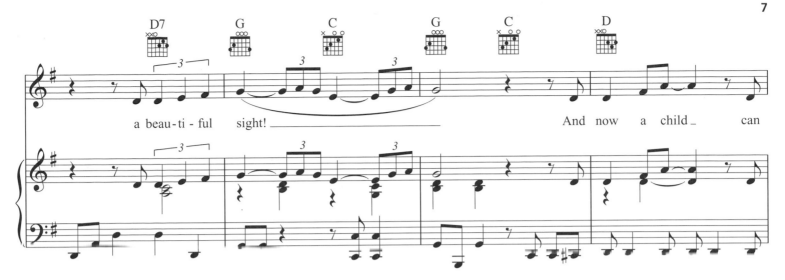

a beau-ti-ful sight! _____ And now a child _ can

un - der - stand _ that this is the law of all the land, all the land! ____

The world is black, the world is white; it turns by day _ and

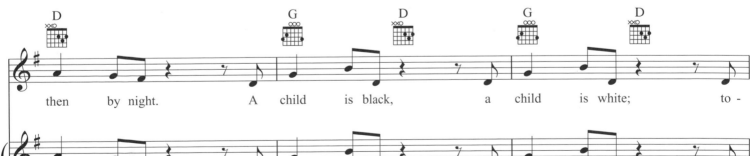

then by night. A child is black, a child is white; to -

BORN TO BE WILD
from EASY RIDER

Words and Music by
MARS BONFIRE

make it hap - pen, take the world in a love em - brace. _

Fire _ all of your guns _ at once _ and ex - plode _ in - to space. _

Like a true _ na - ture child _ we were born, _

born to be wild. _ We have climbed _ so high, _

nev-er want to die. _____ Born to be wild. _

_____ Born to be wild. _

Born to be wild. _____

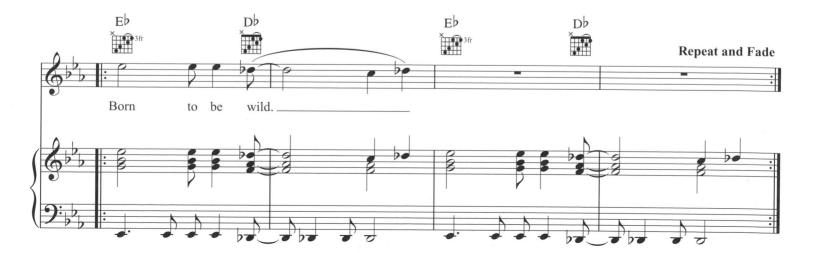

BLACKBIRD

Words and Music by JOHN LENNON
and PAUL McCARTNEY

Slowly and smoothly

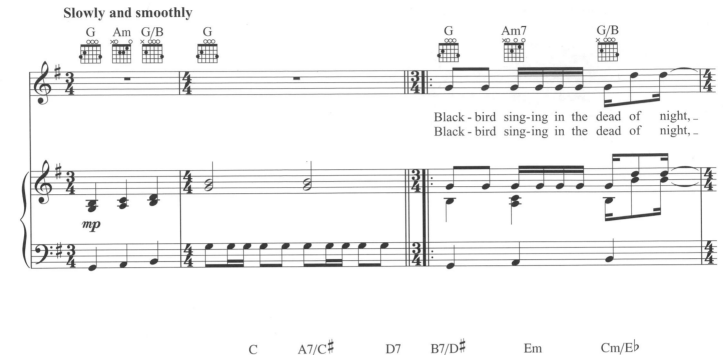

Black-bird sing-ing in the dead of night,_
Black-bird sing-ing in the dead of night,_

take these bro-ken wings_ and learn to fly;_
take these sunk-en eyes_ and learn to see;_

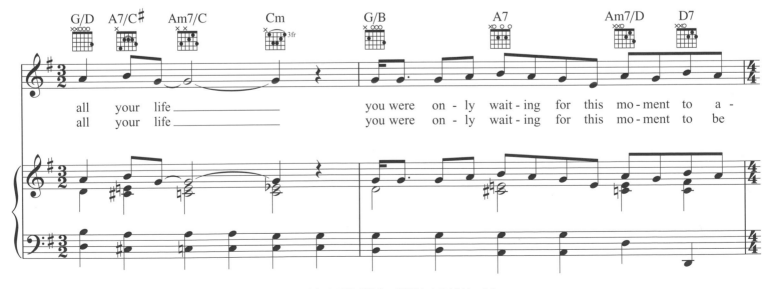

all your life _____ you were on-ly wait-ing for this mo-ment to a-
all your life _____ you were on-ly wait-ing for this mo-ment to be

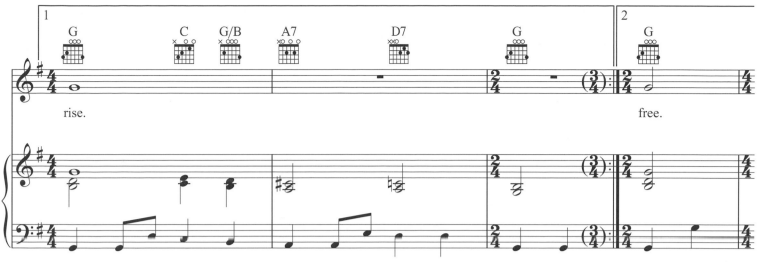

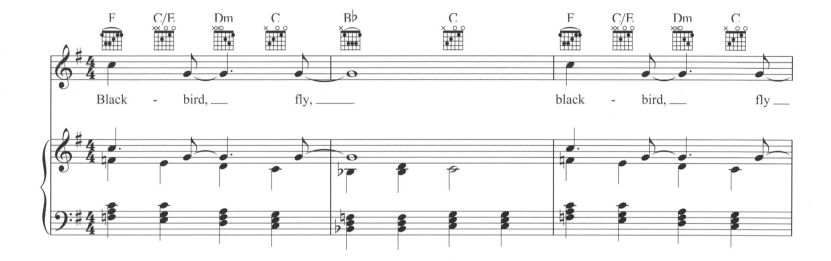

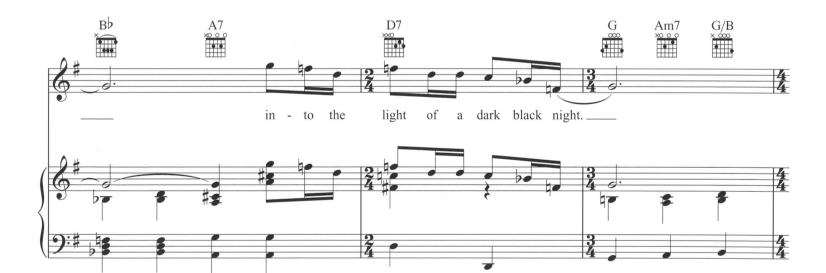

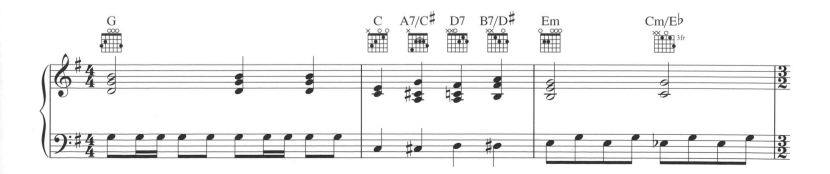

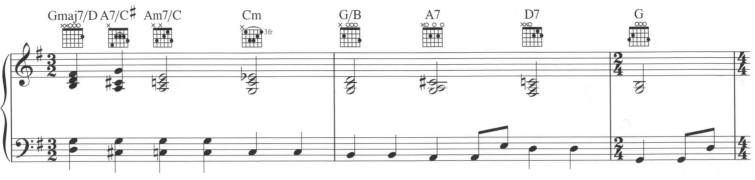

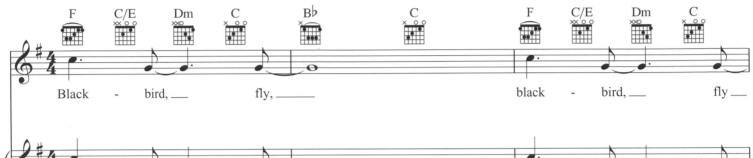

Black - bird, ___ fly, _____ black - bird, ___ fly ___

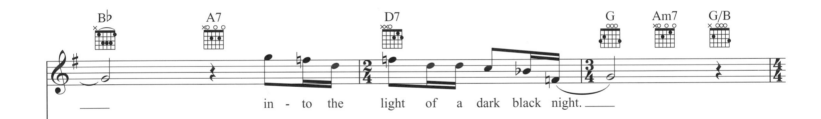

in - to the light of a dark black night. ___

molto rit.   *a tempo*

THE EAGLE AND THE HAWK

Words by JOHN DENVER
Music by JOHN DENVER
and MIKE TAYLOR

Fast, in 2

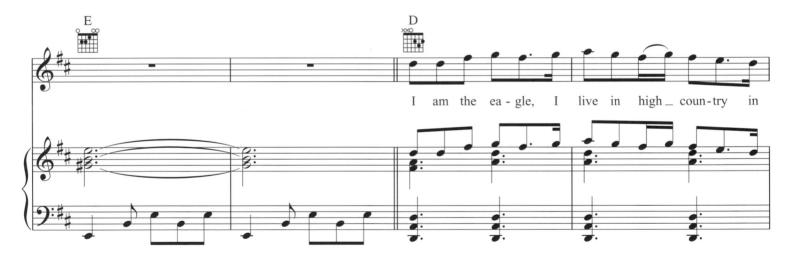

I am the ea-gle, I live in high _ coun-try in

rock-y ca-the-drals that reach to the sky. I am the hawk, and there's

18

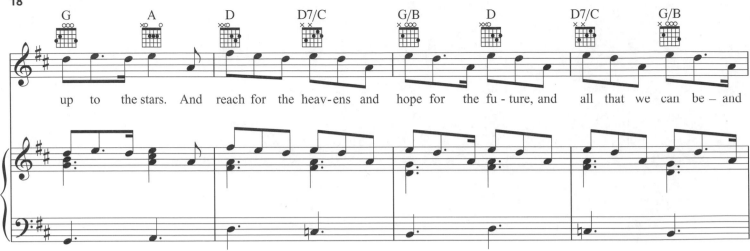

up to the stars. And reach for the heav-ens and hope for the fu-ture, and all that we can be — and

not what we are. _____

sim.

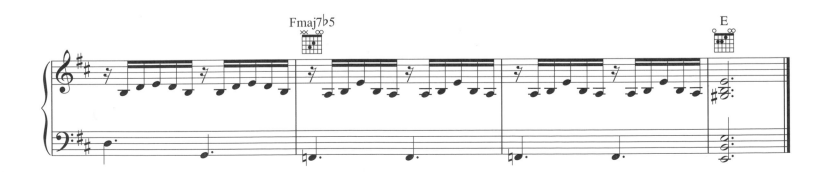

FREE BIRD

Words and Music by ALLEN COLLINS
and RONNIE VAN ZANT

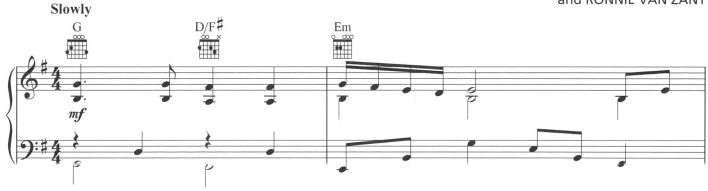

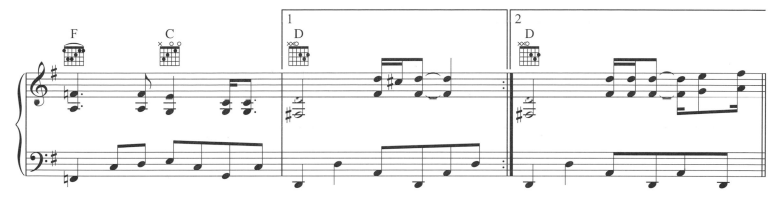

If I leave __ here to - mor - row,   would you still re - mem - ber
Bye, bye, ba - by, it's been a sweet love,   though this feel - ing I can't

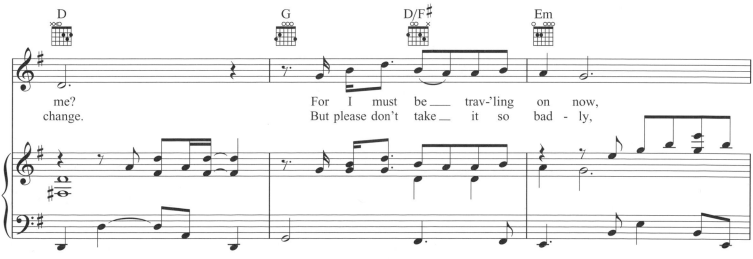

me?   For I must be __ trav - 'ling on now,
change.   But please don't take __ it so bad - ly,

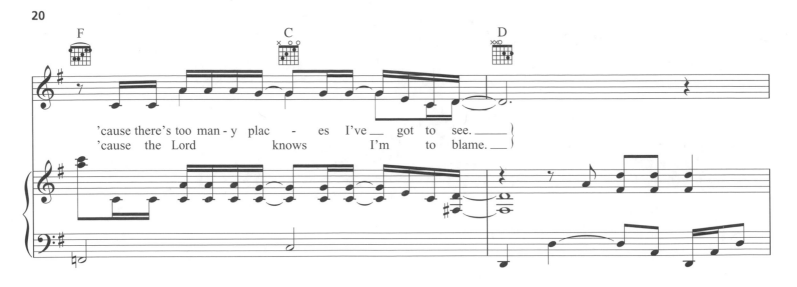

'cause there's too man - y plac - es I've__ got to see.__
'cause the Lord knows I'm to blame.__

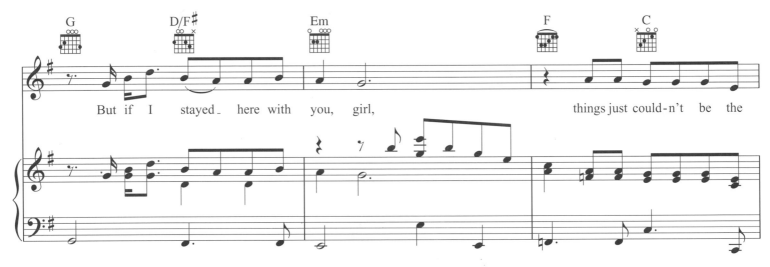

But if I stayed__ here with you, girl, things just could-n't be the

same. 'Cause I'm as free__ as a bird now.

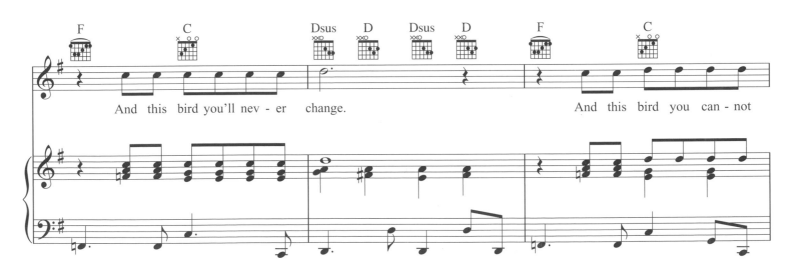

And this bird you'll nev - er change. And this bird you can - not

change. _____   And this bird you can-not   change. _____

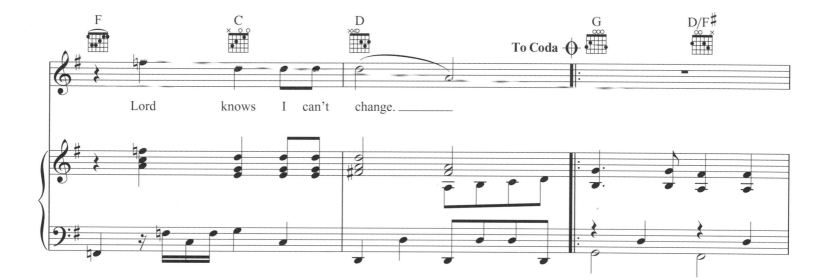

Lord   knows   I   can't   change. _____

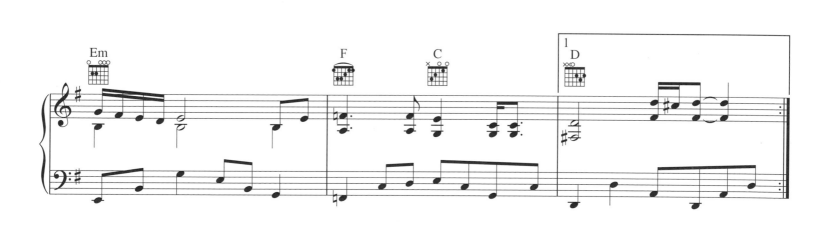

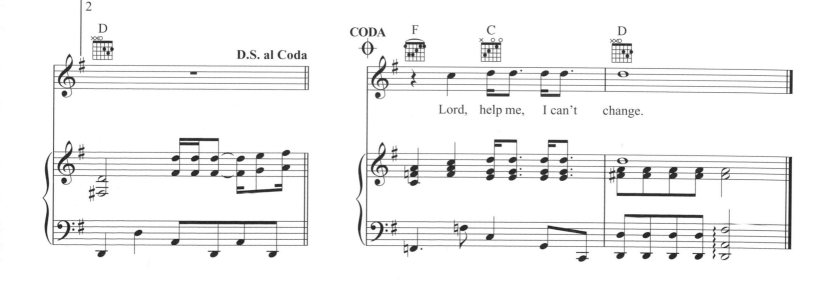

Lord,   help me,   I   can't   change.

FIRE AND RAIN

Words and Music by
JAMES TAYLOR

Slowly

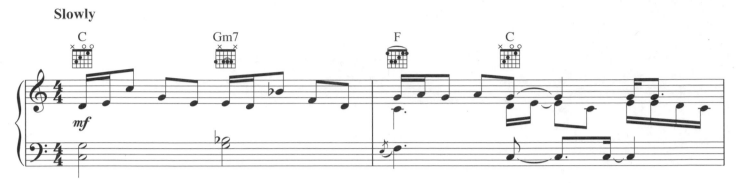

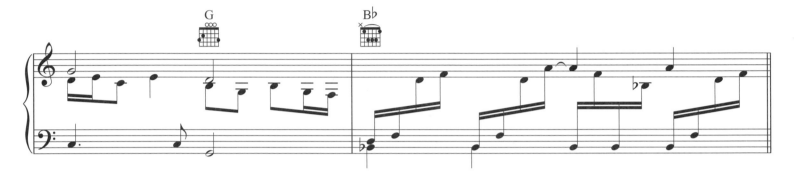

Just yes-ter-day morn-ing they let me know__ you were gone.__
look down up-on me, Je-sus? You got-ta help me make a stand.

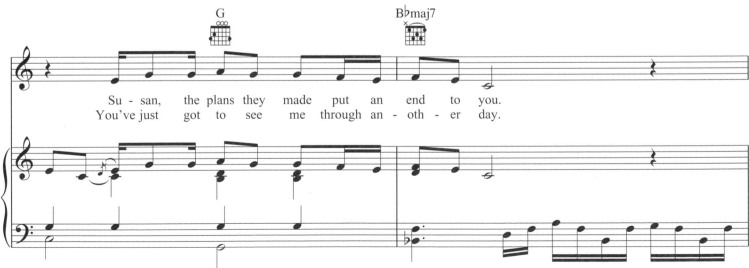

Su-san, the plans they made put an end to you.
You've just got to see me through an-oth-er day.

I walked out this morn - ing and I wrote down this song. __
My bod - y's ach - ing and my time is at hand __

I just can't re - mem - ber who to send __ it to. __
and I __ won't make it an - y oth - er way. __

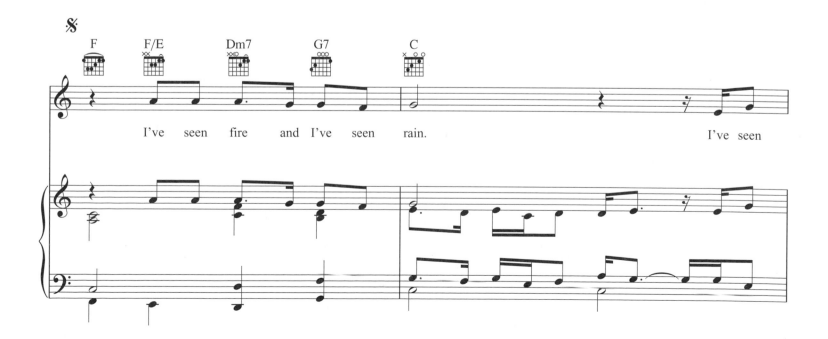

I've seen fire and I've seen rain. I've seen

24

F   F/E   Dm7   G7   C

sun - ny days _ that I thought _ would nev - er end. ___   I've seen

F   F/E   Dm7   G7   C

lone - ly times _ when I could not find a friend, ___   but I

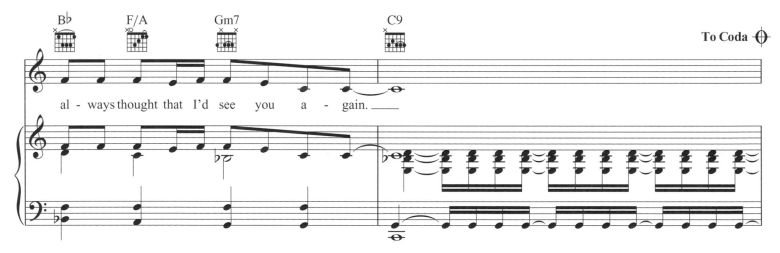

Bb   F/A   Gm7   C9   **To Coda** ⊕

al - ways thought that I'd see you a - gain. ___

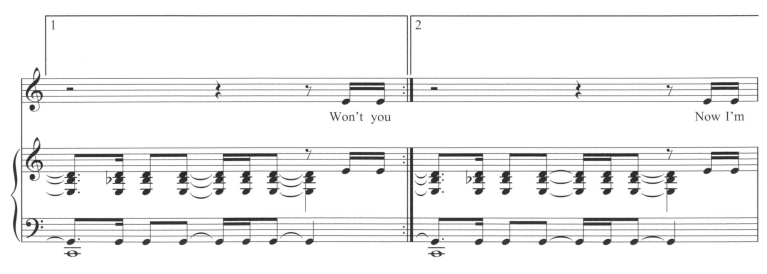

1

Won't you

2

Now I'm

25

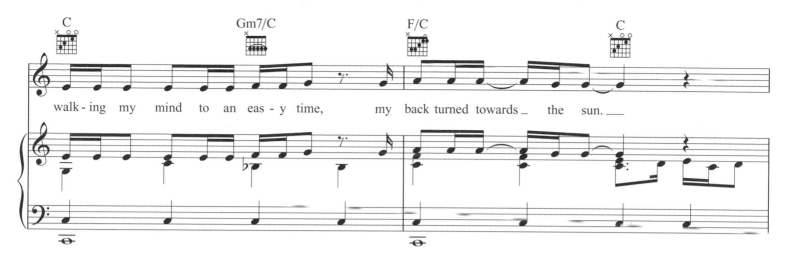

walk-ing my mind to an eas-y time, my back turned towards _ the sun. _

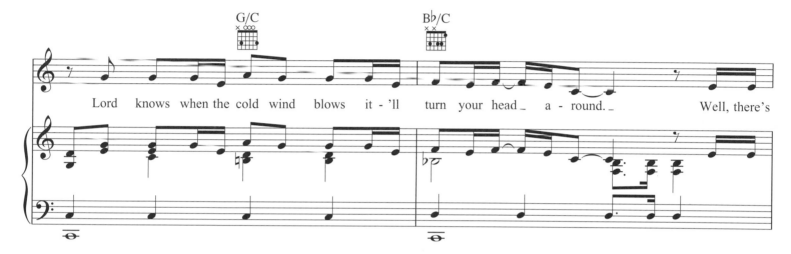

Lord knows when the cold wind blows it-'ll turn your head _ a-round. _ Well, there's

hours of time _ on the tel-e-phone line _ to talk a-bout things to come, _

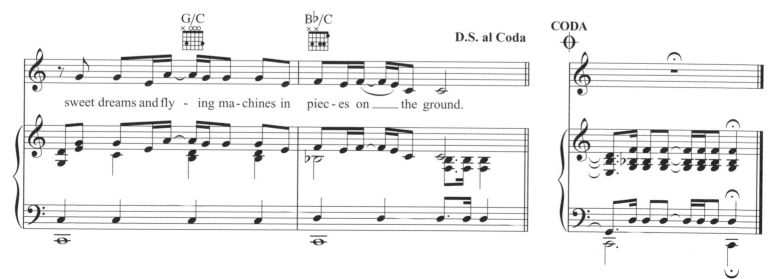

sweet dreams and fly-ing ma-chines in piec-es on _ the ground.

FOR WHAT IT'S WORTH

Words and Music by
STEPHEN STILLS

tell - in' me I've got to be - ware. __

I think it's time we stop. Chil - dren, what's that sound? __

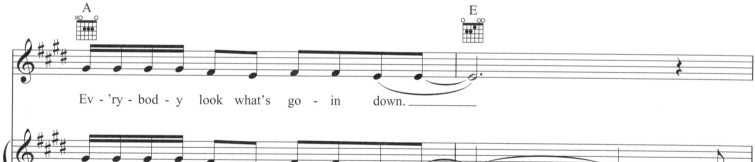

Ev - 'ry - bod - y look what's go - in down. _____

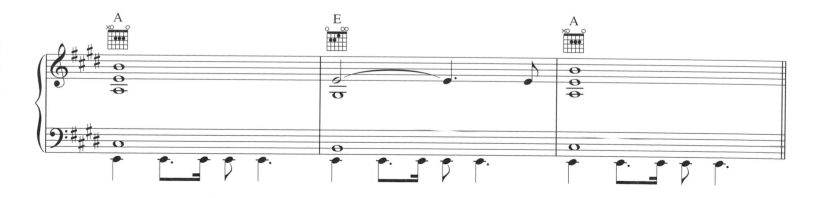

stop. Chil - dren, what's that sound? __ Ev - 'ry - bod - y look what's go - in down. __

take you a - way. __ You bet - ter

stop. Hey, what's that sound? __ Ev - 'ry - bod - y look what's go - in' down. You bet - ter

FREE AS A BIRD

Words and Music by
JOHN LENNON

Slow, steady Rock

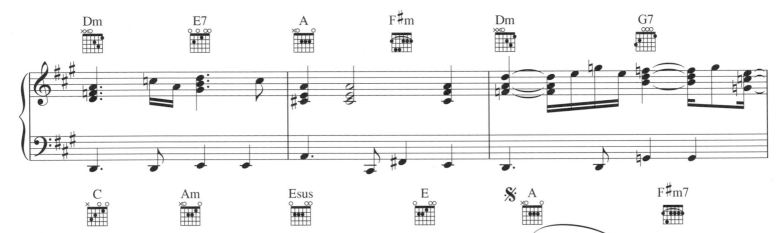

(D.S.) Free
Home, _____

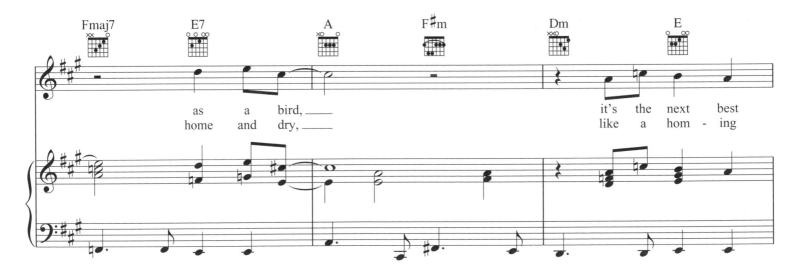

as a bird, _____   it's the next best
home and dry, _____   like a hom - ing

thing to be ____ free ___ as a bird.
bird I fly, ____ as a bird on wings.

What-ev-er hap-pened to ___ the life that we once knew?

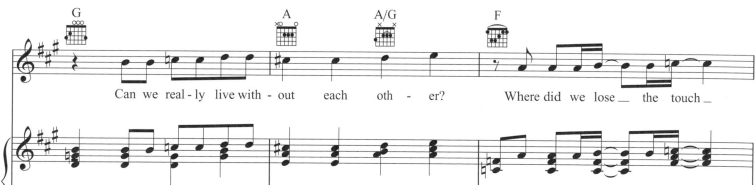

Can we real-ly live with-out each oth-er? Where did we lose __ the touch __

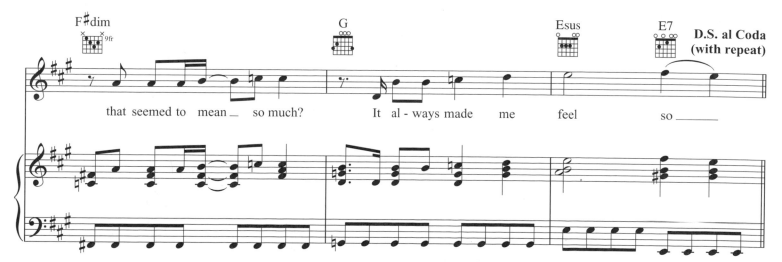

that seemed to mean __ so much? It al-ways made me feel so _____

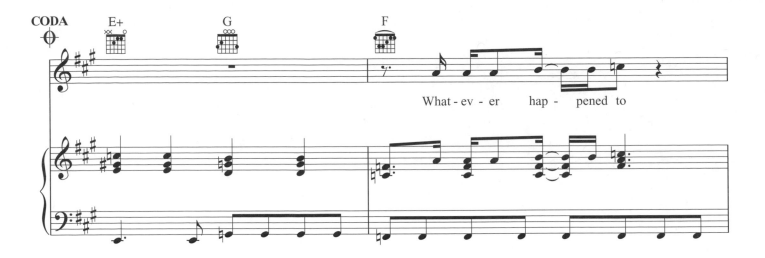

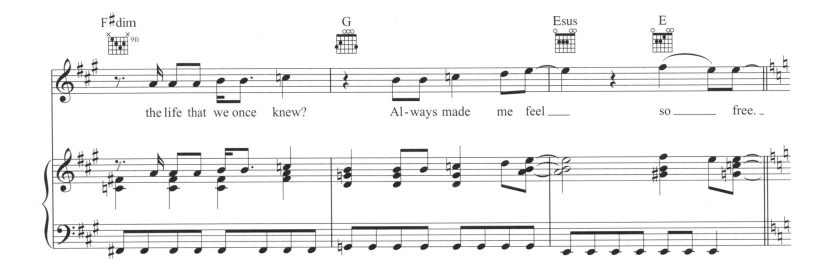

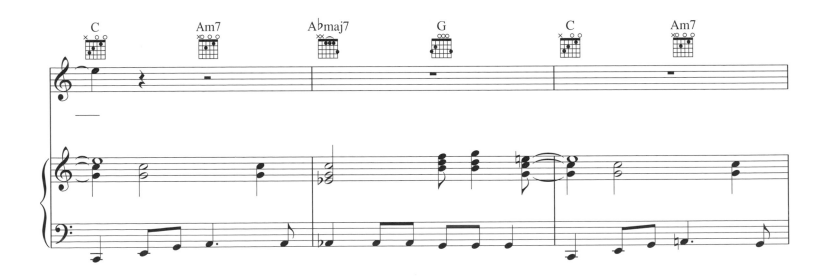

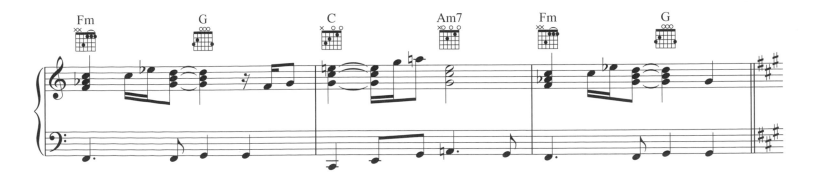

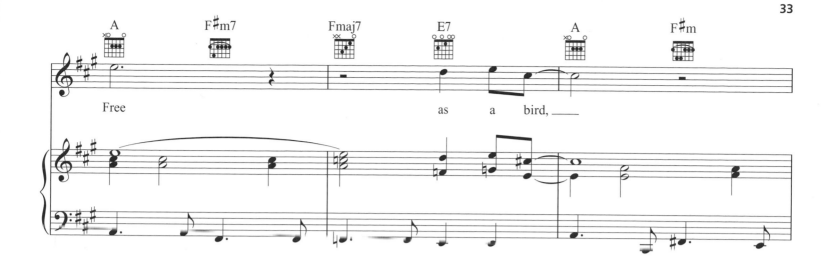

Free   as   a   bird, _____

It's the next best thing to be _____   free ___ as   a

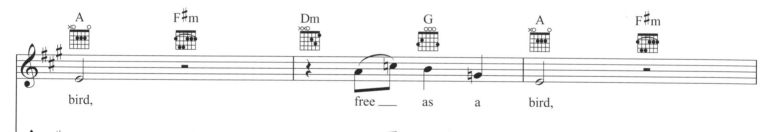

bird,   free ___ as   a   bird,

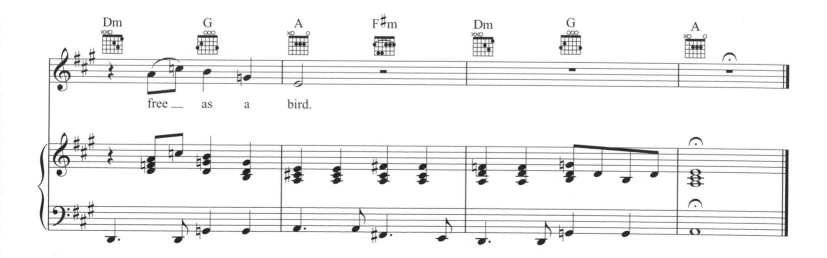

free ___ as   a   bird.

A HORSE WITH NO NAME

Words and Music by
DEWEY BUNNELL

36

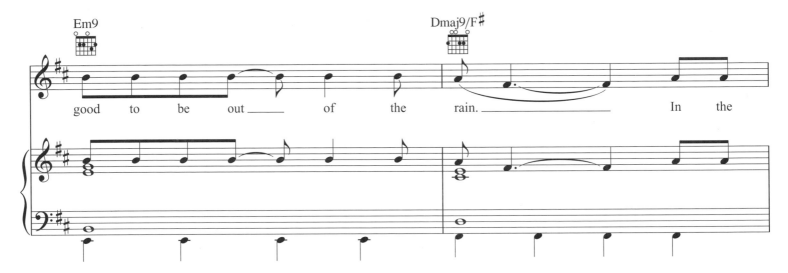

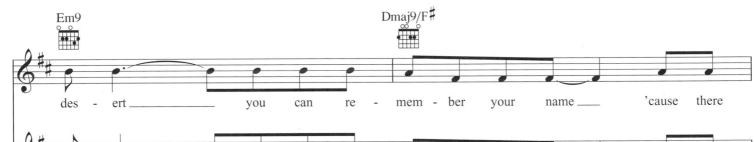

To Coda

38

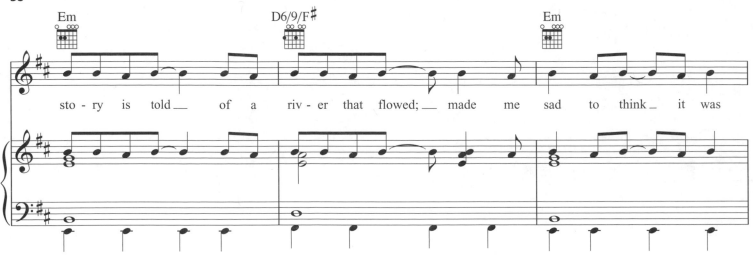

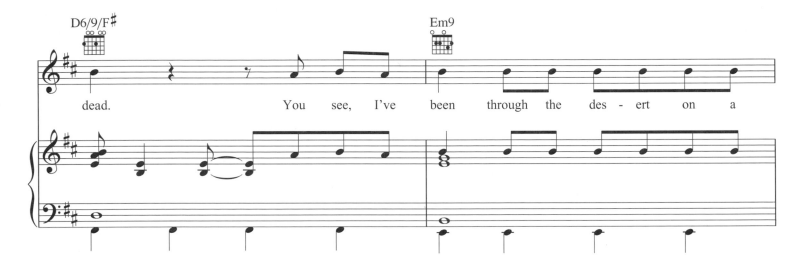

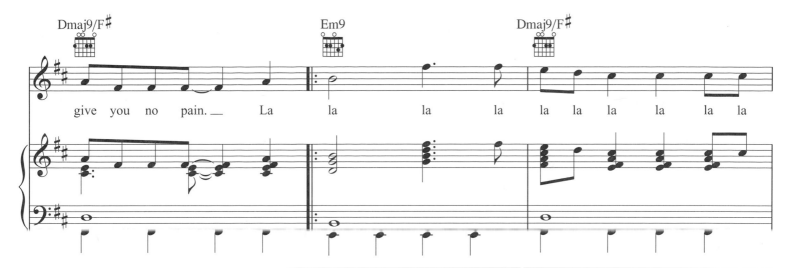

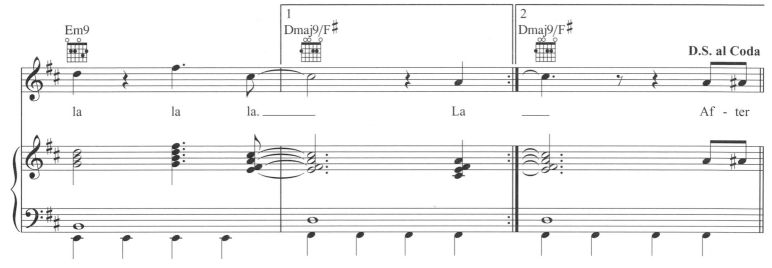

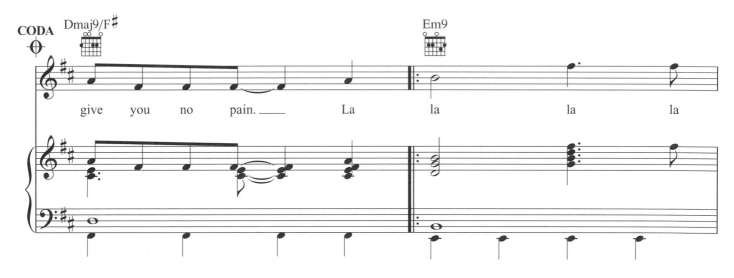

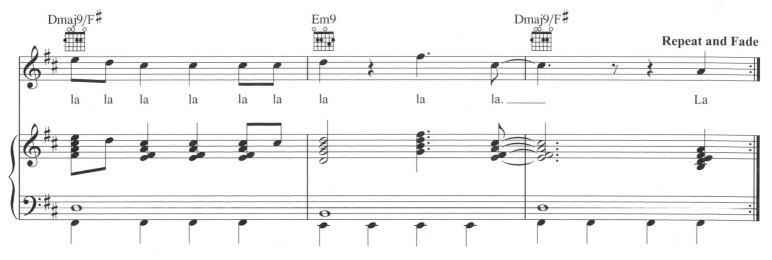

I GOT A NAME

Words by NORMAN GIMBEL
Music by CHARLES FOX

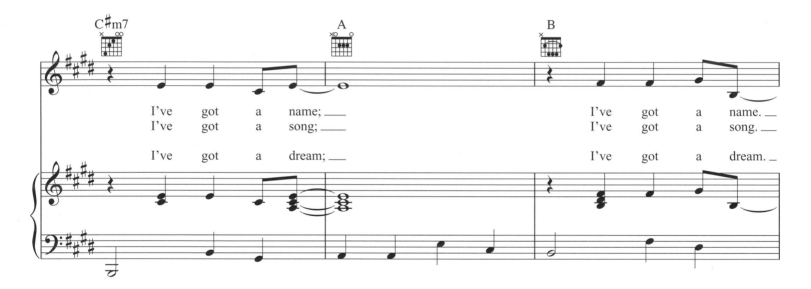

and the croak - ing toad,   I've got a name: ___
and the ba - by's cry,   I've got a song; ___

but they can't change me,   I've got a dream; ___

To Coda I

I've got a name, ___
I've got a song, ___

I've got a dream. ___

Instrumental ends

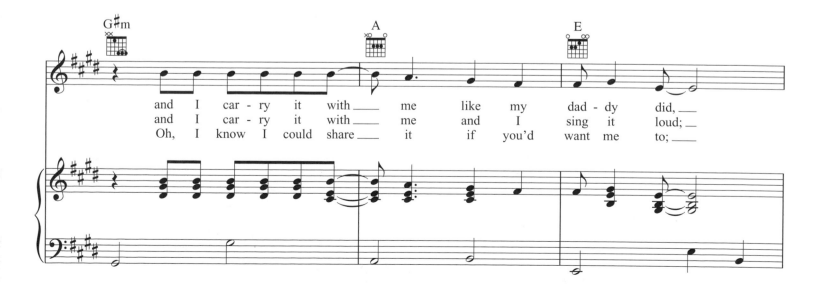

and I car - ry it with ___ me   like my dad - dy did, ___
and I car - ry it with ___ me   and I sing it loud; ___
Oh, I know I could share ___ it   if you'd want me to; ___

D.C. al Coda II

CODA I

And I'm gon - na go ___ there free. _____

CODA II

___ Mov-in' me down the high - way, roll-in' me down the high-

- way, mov-in' a - head so life ___ won't pass ___ me by. ___

a tempo

I'D LOVE TO CHANGE THE WORLD

Words and Music by
ALVIN LEE

Bright Folk Rock

Ev - 'ry-where there's
Pop - u - la - tion

freaks __ and hair - ies,
keeps __ on breed-ing,

dykes __ and fair - ies.
na - tion bleed-ing,

Tell __ me, where is
still __ more feed-ing

them and us, _____ stop the war. _

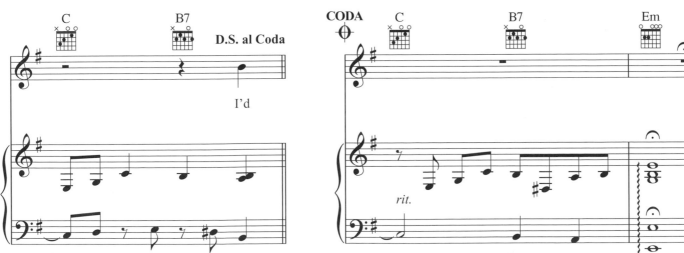

D.S. al Coda

I'd

CODA

rit.

LAY DOWN
(Candles in the Rain)

Words and Music by
MELANIE SAFKA

Slow Gospel Rock

Lay down, lay down, lay it all down, let your white birds smile up at the ones who stand _ and frown. Lay down, lay down, lay it all down, let your white birds smile up at the ones who stand _ and frown.

50

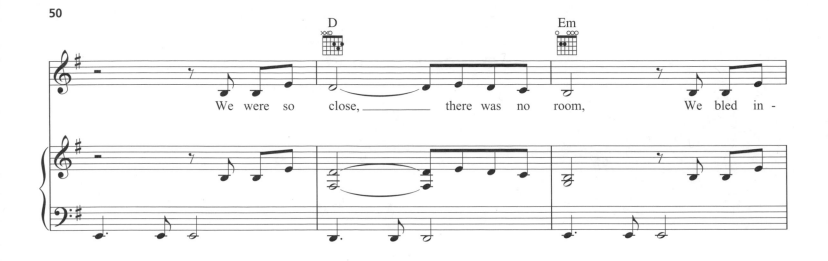

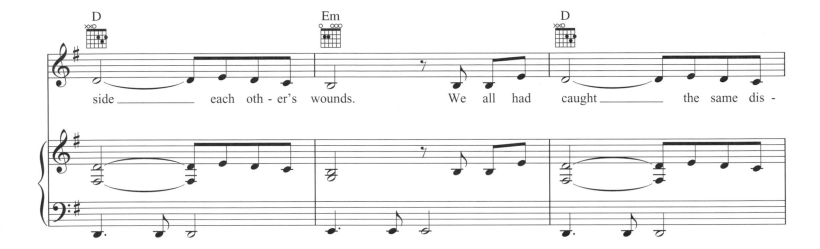

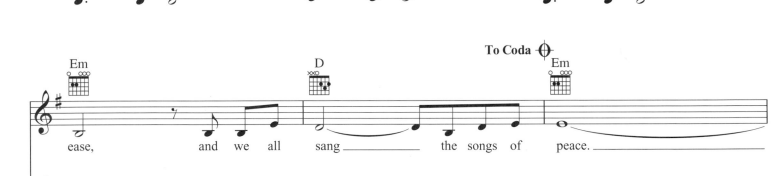

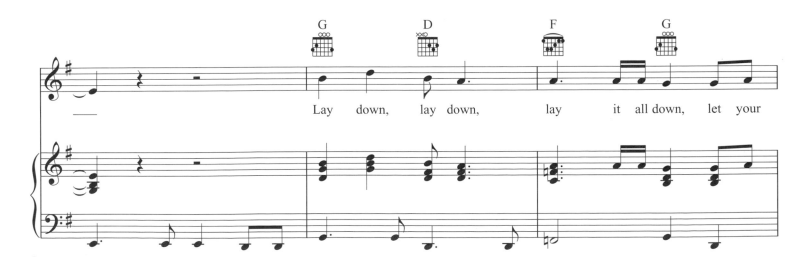

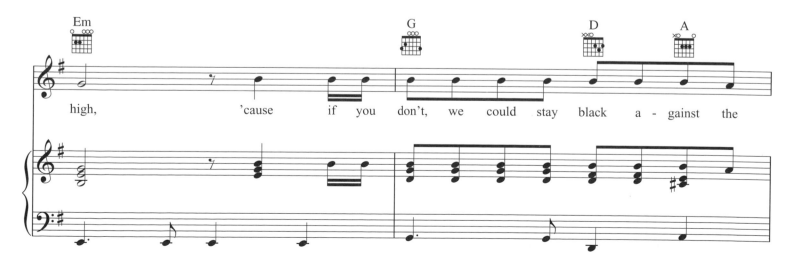

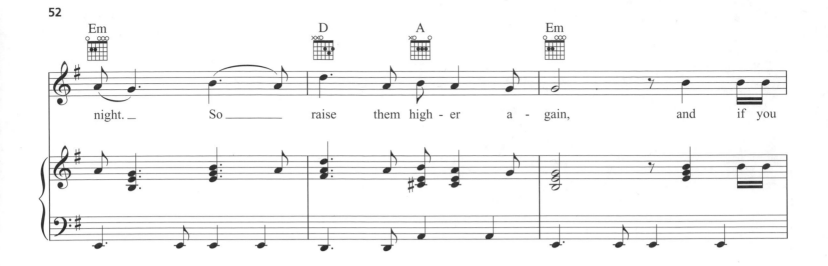

night. _ So _____ raise them high - er a - gain, and if you

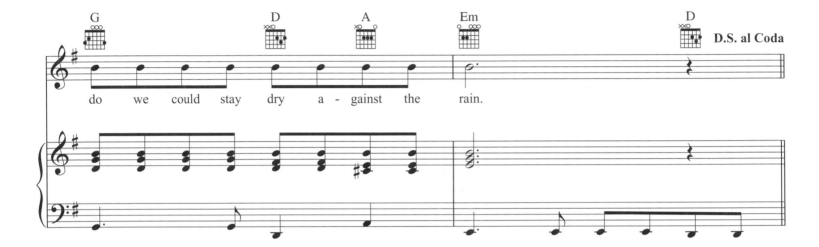

do we could stay dry a - gainst the rain.

D.S. al Coda

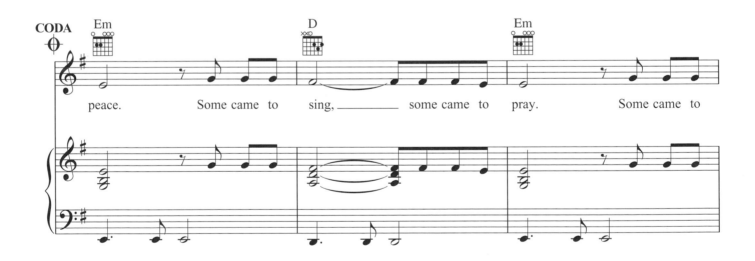

CODA

peace. Some came to sing, _____ some came to pray. Some came to

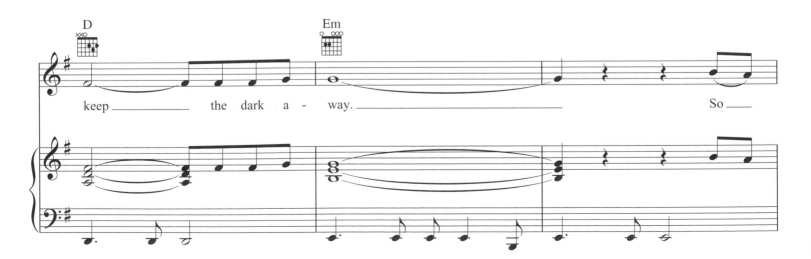

keep _____ the dark a - way. _____ So ___

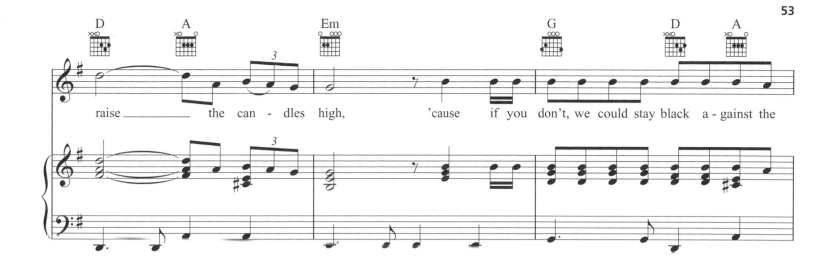

raise _____ the can - dles high, 'cause if you don't, we could stay black a - gainst the

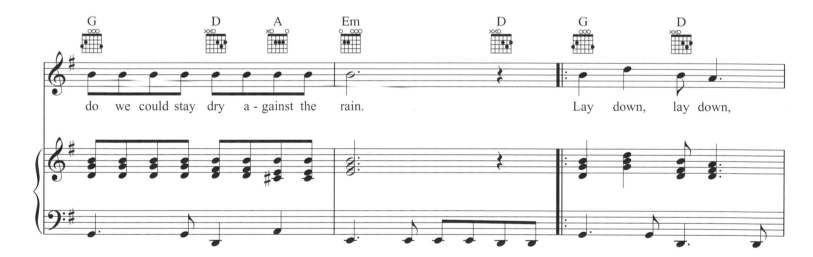

night. _ So _____ raise them high - er a - gain, and if you

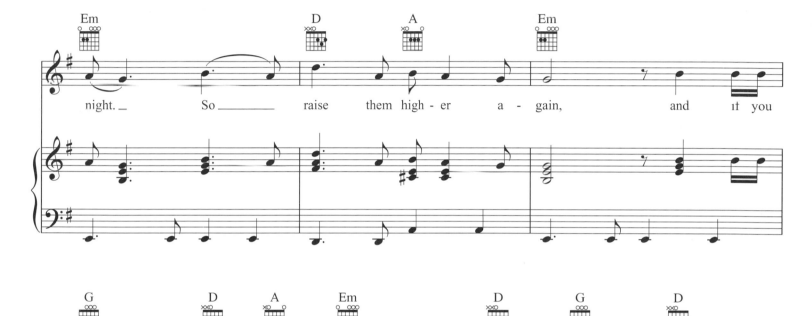

do we could stay dry a - gainst the rain. Lay down, lay down,

lay it all down, let your white birds smile up at the ones who stand _ and frown. You got to

IF I HAD A HAMMER
(The Hammer Song)

Words and Music by LEE HAYS
and PETE SEEGER

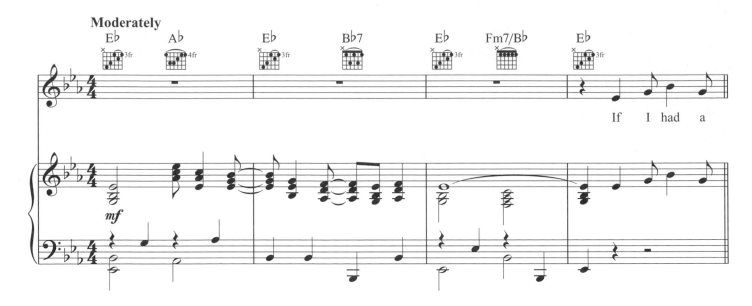

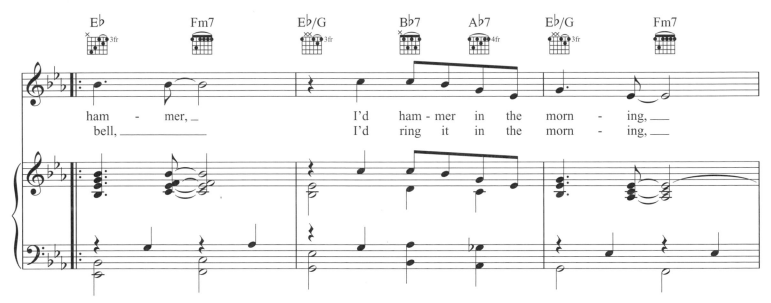

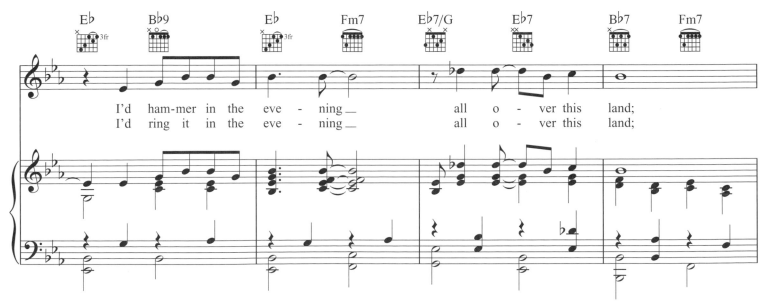

I'd ham-mer out dan - ger, __ I'd ham-mer out a warn - ing, __
I'd ring __ out dan - ger, __ I'd ring __ out a warn - ing, __

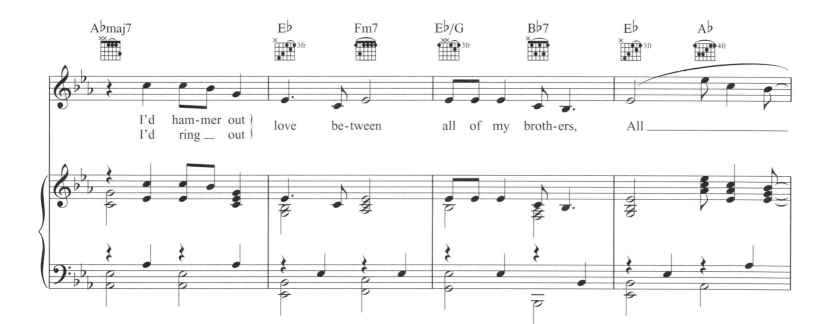

I'd ham-mer out } love be-tween all of my broth-ers, All ____
I'd ring __ out }

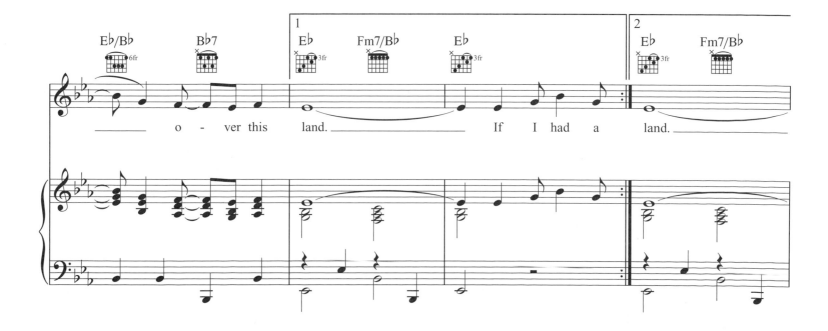

____ o - ver this land. ____ If I had a land.

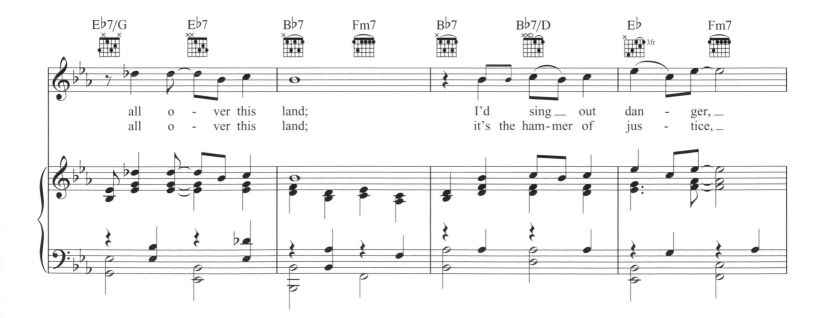

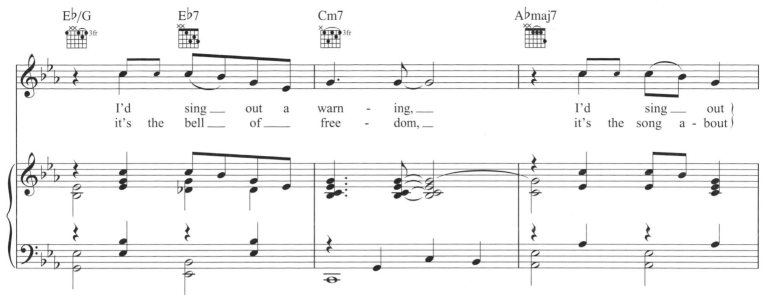

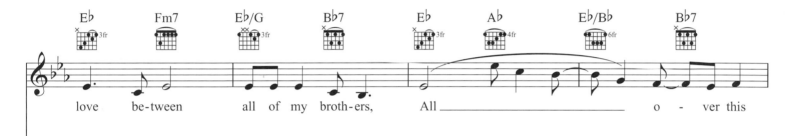

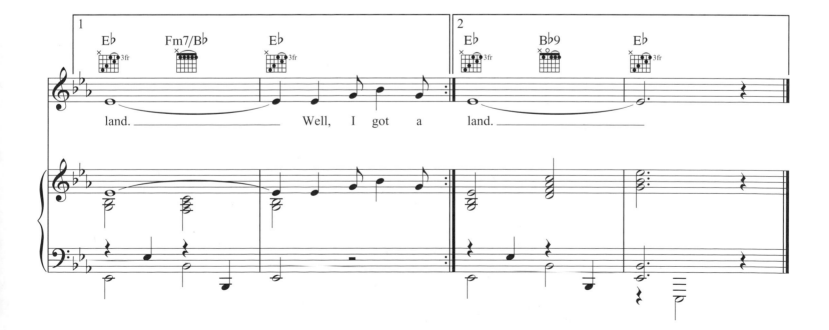

IMAGINE

Words and Music by
JOHN LENNON

Slowly

I-mag-ine there's no heav-en. ___ It's eas-y if you ___ try. ___ No hell ___ be-low us, a-bove us on-ly sky. ___

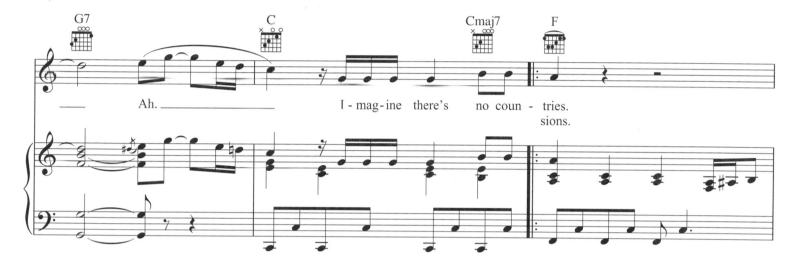

and no re - li - gion, ___ too. _____
a broth - er - hood ___ of man. _____

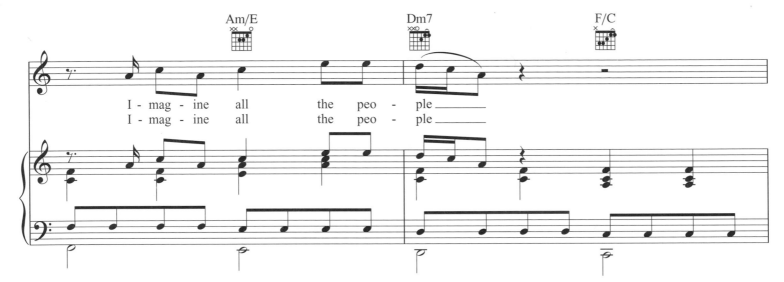

I - mag - ine all the peo - ple _____
I - mag - ine all the peo - ple _____

liv - ing life in peace. ___ ⎱ You, _____ you may say _____ I'm a
shar - ing all the world. ___ ⎰

dream - er, but I'm not the on - ly one. __

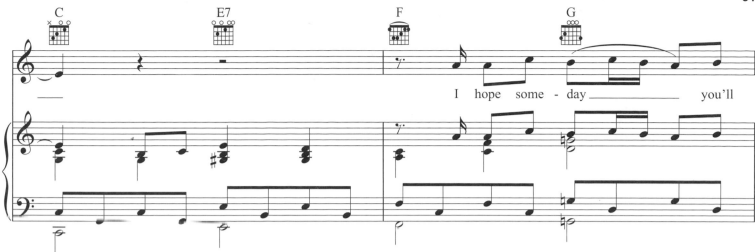
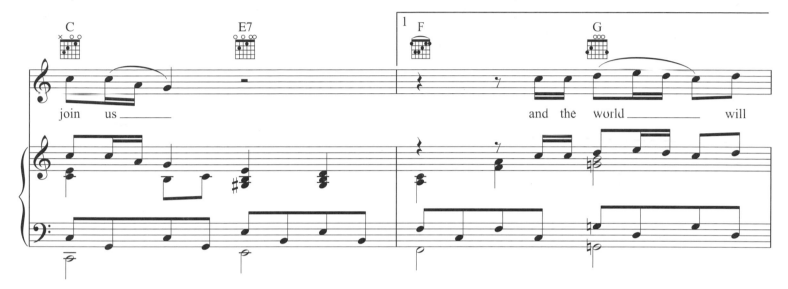
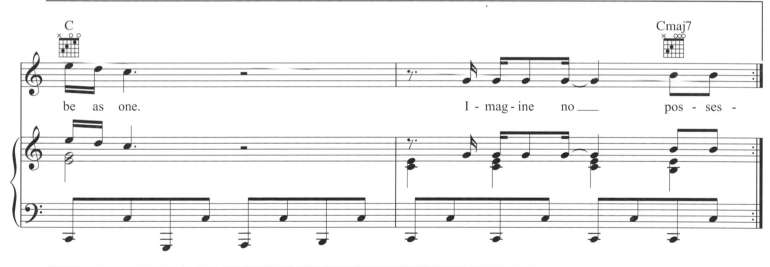

LET'S GET TOGETHER

(Get Together)

Words and Music by
CHET POWERS

Love is but the
Some will come and
If you heard the

song   we sing,   and fear's   the way   we   die. _____
some   will go,   and we   shall sure - ly   pass. _____
song   I sing,   you   must un - der - stand. _____

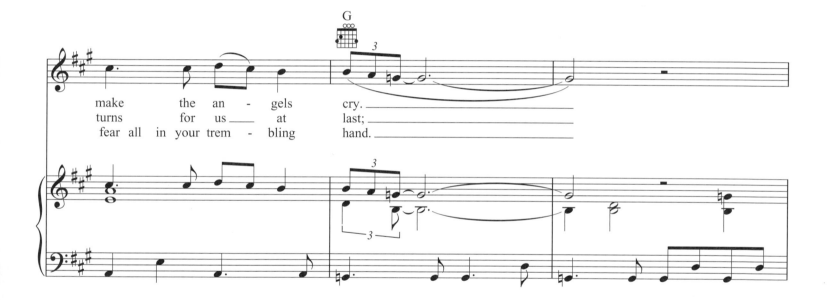

64

why. _____
grass. _____
mand. _____

C'-mon peo-ple now, smile _

on your broth-er. Let's _____ get to-geth-er, try and love one an-oth-er, right

To Coda ⊕ | 1, 2 | 3 |

D.S. al Coda

now. _____

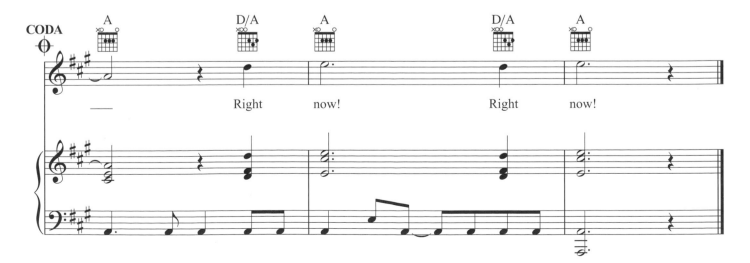

CODA

Right now! Right now!

LIFT EV'RY VOICE AND SING

Words by JAMES WELDON JOHNSON
Music by J. ROSAMOND JOHNSON

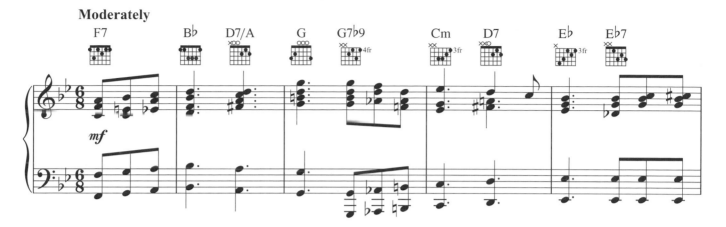

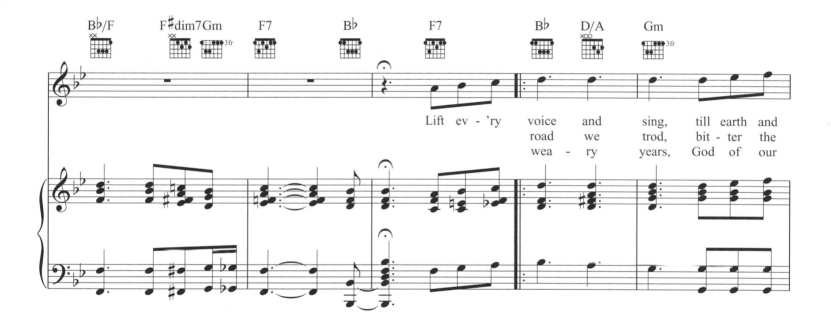

Lift ev - 'ry voice and sing, till earth and
road we trod, bit - ter the
wea - ry years, God of our

heav - en ring, ring with the har - mo - nies of
chast - 'ning rod, felt in the days when hope un -
si - lent tears, Thou who hast brought us thus far

lib - er - ty; Let our re - joic - ing rise high as the
born _____ had died; Yet with a stead - y beat, have not our
on _____ the way; Thou who hast by Thy might led us in -

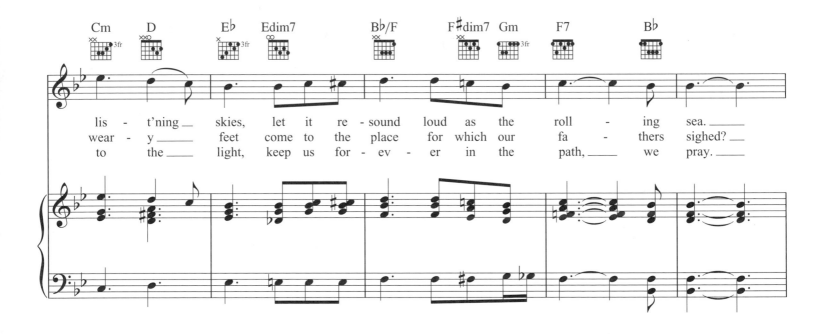

lis - t'ning __ skies, let it re - sound loud as the roll - ing sea. _____
wear - y __ feet come to the place for which our fa - thers sighed? __
to the __ light, keep us for - ev - er in the path, _____ we pray. _____

Sing a song full of the faith that the dark past has taught us.
We have come o - ver a - way that with tears has been wa - tered.
Lest our feet stray from the plac - es, our God, where we met Thee,

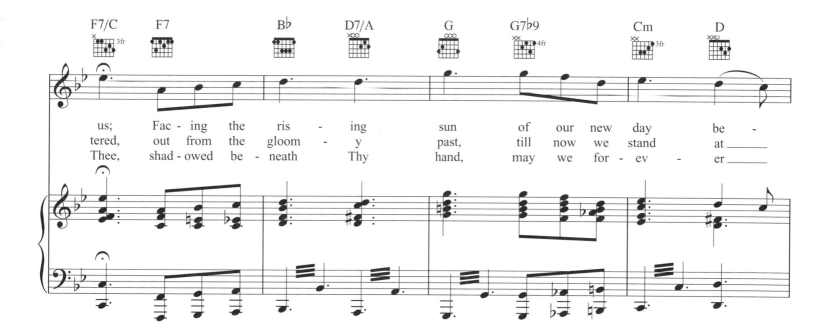

LOVE TRAIN

Words and Music by KENNETH GAMBLE
and LEON HUFF

Peo - ple all o - ver the world, join hands, start a love train, love train. Peo - ple all o - ver the world, join hands,

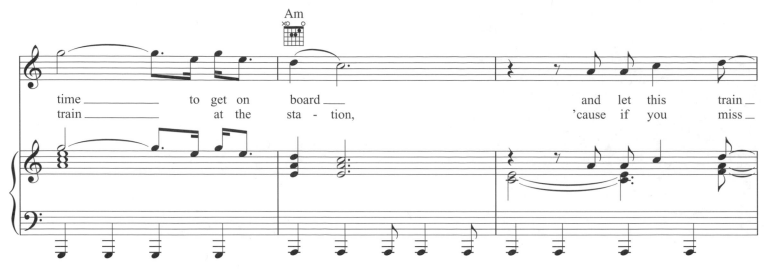

time _____ to get on board _____ and let this train _
train _____ at the sta - tion, 'cause if you miss _

_ keep on rid - in', rid - in' on
_ I feel sor - ry, sor - ry for

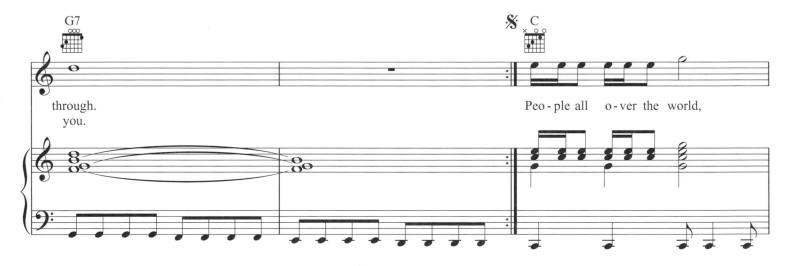

through. Peo - ple all o - ver the world,
you.

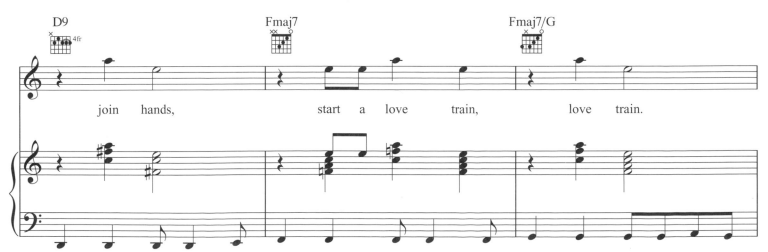

join hands, start a love train, love train.

D.S. and Fade

ME AND BOBBY McGEE

Words and Music by KRIS KRISTOFFERSON
and FRED FOSTER

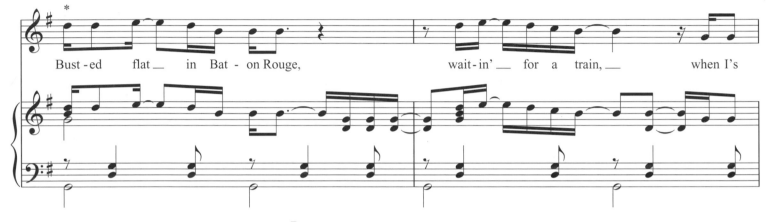

Busted flat in Baton Rouge, waitin' for a train, when I's feel-in' near as fad-ed as my jeans. Bob-by thumbed a die-sel down just be-fore it rained. It rode us all the way in-to New Or-leans. I

* *Vocal written one octave higher than sung.*

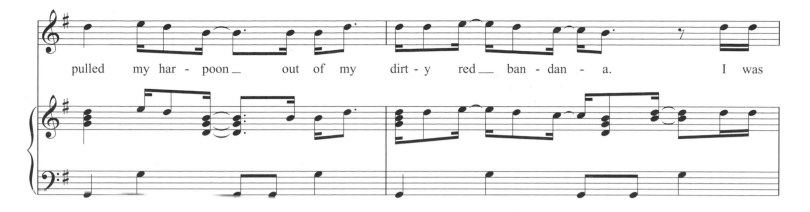

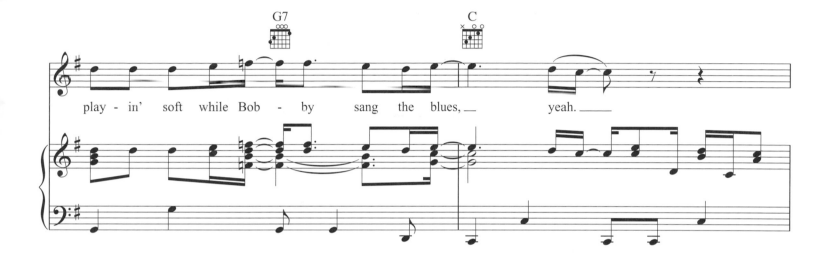

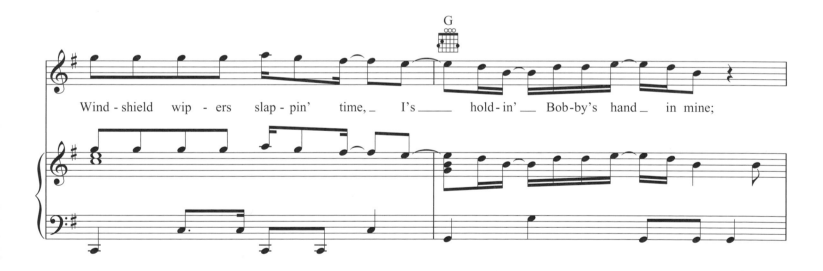

noth-in' left to lose. ___ Noth-in', I mean noth-in', hon', if it ain't

free, ___ no, no. ___ Yeah, feel-in' good was eas-y, Lord, ___

___ when he ___ sang the blues. ___ You know, feel-in' good was good e-nough ___ for me, ___

good e-nough ___ for me ___ an' my Bob-by Mc-Gee.

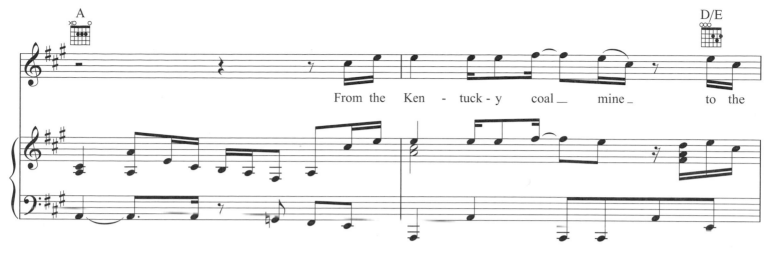

From the Ken - tuck - y coal mine to the

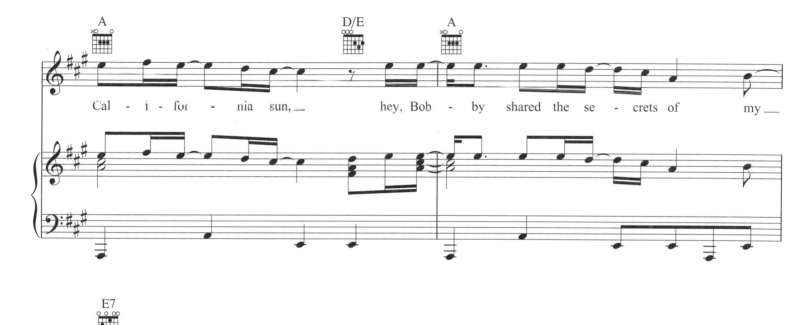

Cal - i - for - nia sun, hey, Bob - by shared the se - crets of my soul.

Through all kinds of weath - er, through

ev - 'ry - thing we done, yeah, Bob - by ba - by kept me from the cold.

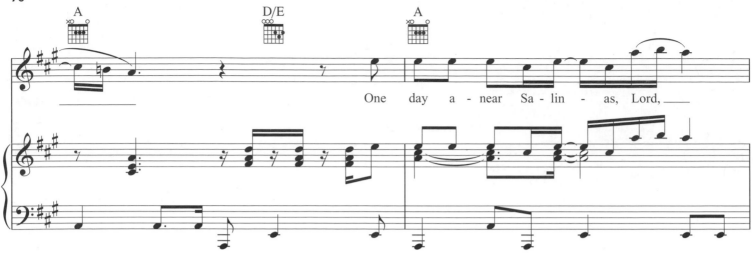

One day a - near Sa - lin - as, Lord,

I let him slip a - way. He's look - in' for that home and I hope he

finds it. But I'd trade all of my to - mor - rows for one

sin - gle yes - ter - day to be hold - in' Bob - by's bod - y next to mine.

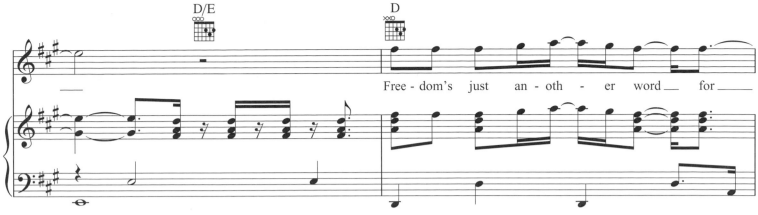

Free-dom's just an-oth-er word_ for_

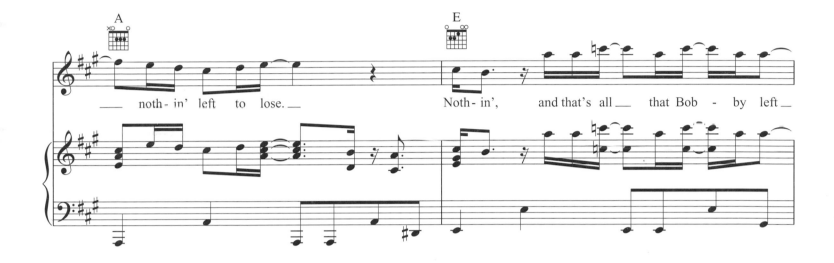

_ noth-in' left to lose. _ Noth-in', and that's all _ that Bob-by left_

_ me, _ yeah. _ But if feel-in' good was eas - y, Lord, _

_ when he _ sang the blues, _ hey, feel-in' good was good e-nough_ for me,_

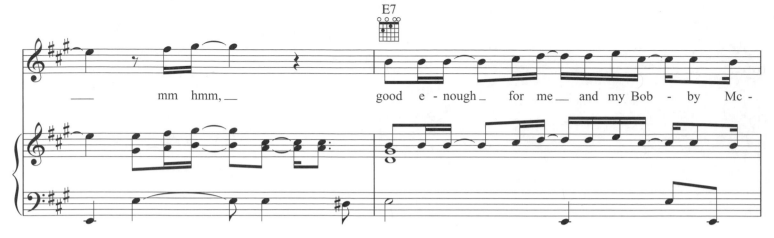

mm hmm, ___ good e-nough ___ for me ___ and my Bob - by Mc-

Gee. La da da da, la da da da, la da da da da da da da, ___

la da da da la ___ da la da Bob-by ___ Mc-Gee, ___ yeah. ___ La da la la la ___ la,

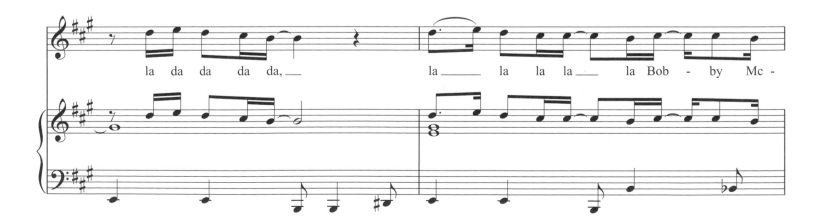

la da da da da, ___ la ___ la la la ___ la Bob - by Mc-

Gee. _____ La da da la da da la__ da da la__ da da, _____

___ la da lo la__ da da la__ da la, hey now, Bob - by, lo now, Bob-by Mc-Gee,__

___ yeah.__ Lo na lo__ na na lo__ na, na,____ lo na na na__

___ na na na__ na na na__ na na na__ na na,____ hey now, Bob - by, lo now, Bob-by Mc- Gee,__

Lord.

La la la___ la la___ la la___ la la___ la la___

___ la la___ la la,___ hey, hey, hey, Bob-by Mc - Gee,___ ah.

ME AND YOU
AND A DOG NAMED BOO

Words and Music by
LOBO

af - ter the sum - mer rain.
rob - bin' from an old hen. ___
- tlin' down in my brain. ___

Will -
Old Mac -
Though it's

pow - er made that old car go, ___
Don - ald, he made us work, ___
on - ly been a month or so, ___

a wom - an's
but then he
that old car's

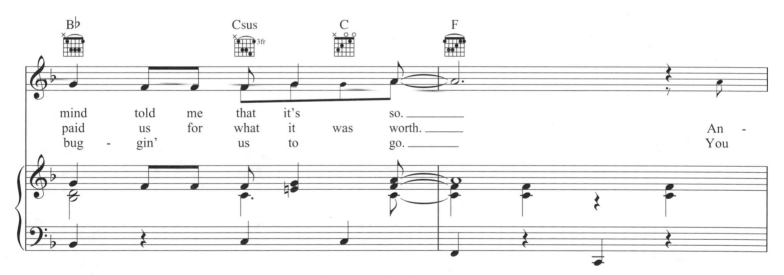

mind told me that it's so. ___
paid us for what it was worth. ___
bug - gin' us to go. ___

An -
You

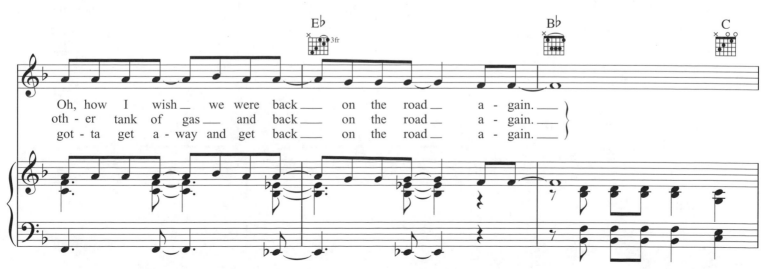

Oh, how I wish ___ we were back ___ on the road ___ a - gain. ___
oth - er tank of gas ___ and back ___ on the road ___ a - gain. ___
got - ta get a - way and get back ___ on the road ___ a - gain. ___

Me and you ___ and a dog ___ named Boo, ___

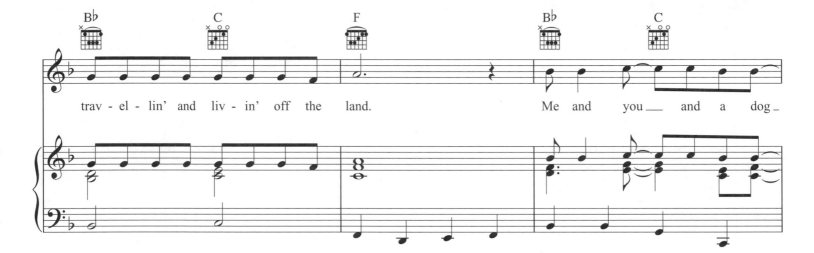

trav - el - lin' and liv - in' off the land. Me and you ___ and a dog ___

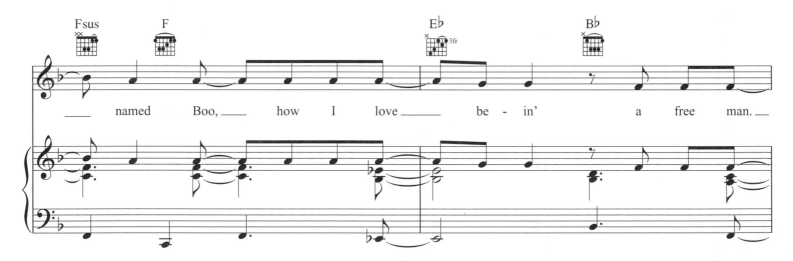

___ named Boo, ___ how I love ___ be - in' a free man. ___

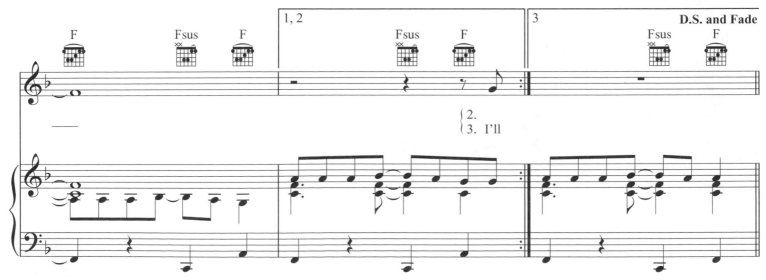

2.
3. I'll

ONE TIN SOLDIER

from BILLY JACK

Words and Music by DENNIS LAMBERT
and BRIAN POTTER

Moderately slow Rock tempo

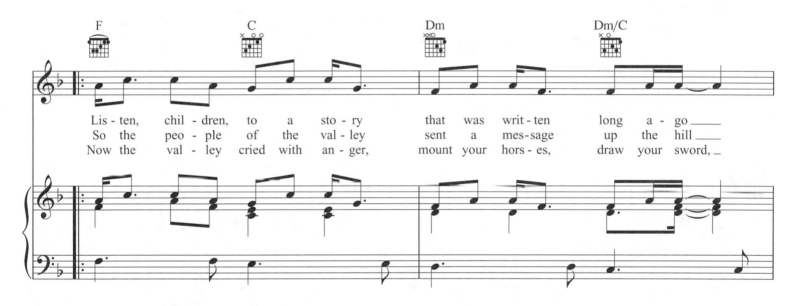

Lis- ten, chil- dren, to a sto- ry   that was writ- ten   long a- go
So the peo- ple of the val- ley   sent a mes- sage   up the hill
Now the val- ley cried with an- ger,   mount your hors- es,   draw your sword,

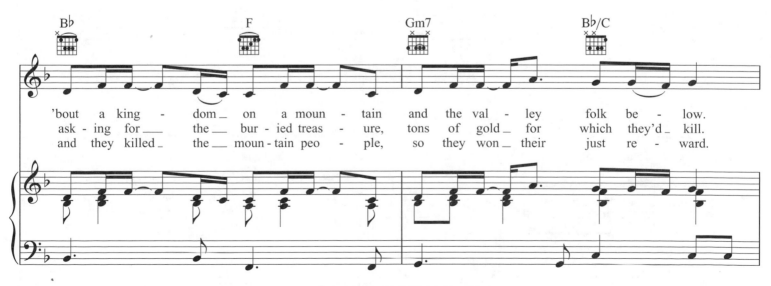

'bout a king- dom on a moun- tain   and the val- ley   folk be- low.
ask- ing for the bur- ied treas- ure,   tons of gold for   which they'd kill.
and they killed the moun- tain peo- ple,   so they won their   just re- ward.

Jus - ti - fy it in the end. __ There won't be an - y trum-pets blow - in'

come the judg - ment day. On the blood - y morn - ing af - ter, _____

____ one tin sol - dier rides a - way. ___

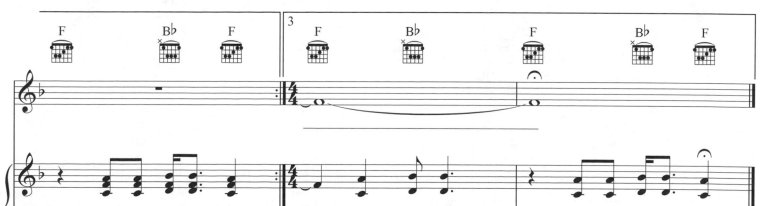

PEOPLE GET READY

Words and Music by
CURTIS MAYFIELD

There ain't no room _ for the hope-less sin-ner _____ who would

hurt all ___ man-kind _ just to save _ his own. _ Have pit-y on those _ whose

D.S. al Coda

choic-es grow thin-ner so there's no hid-ing place _ from the king-dom's throne. _

I'm get-ting read - y. I'm get-ting

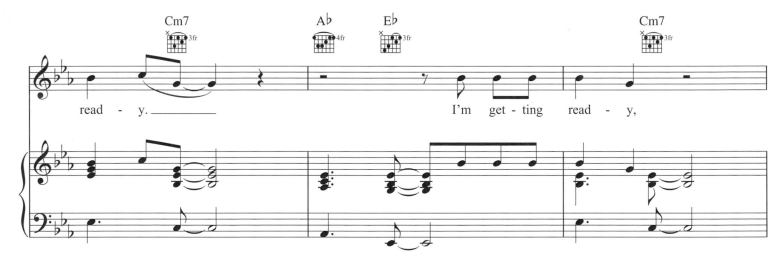

read - y. I'm get-ting read - y,

this time I'm read - y.

PEOPLE GOT TO BE FREE

Words and Music by FELIX CAVALIERE
and EDWARD BRIGATI, JR.

Bright Rock

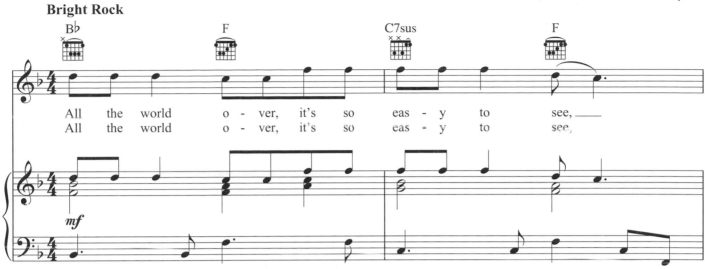

All the world o-ver, it's so eas-y to see,___
All the world o-ver, it's so eas-y to see,

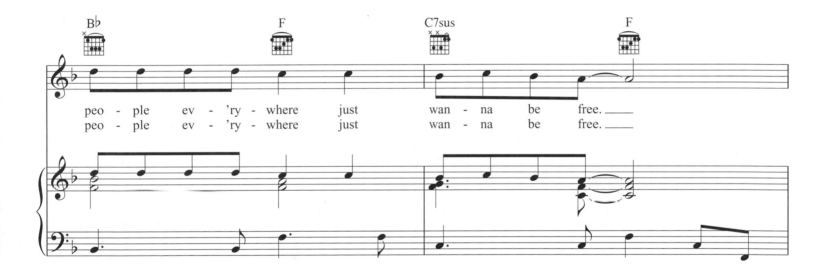

peo-ple ev-'ry-where just wan-na be free.___
peo-ple ev-'ry-where just wan-na be free.___

Lis-ten, please lis-ten, that's the way it should be,___
Can't un-der-stand, it's so___ sim-ple to me,

peace in the val - ley, peo - ple got to be free. _____
peo - ple ev - 'ry - where _ just _ got to be free. _____

You should see _____ what a love - ly, love - ly world this would be _____
If there's a man _____ who is down and needs a help - ing hand, _

_____ if ev - er - y - one _____ learned to live to - geth -
_____ all it takes is you to un - der - stand _____ and to pull him through. _

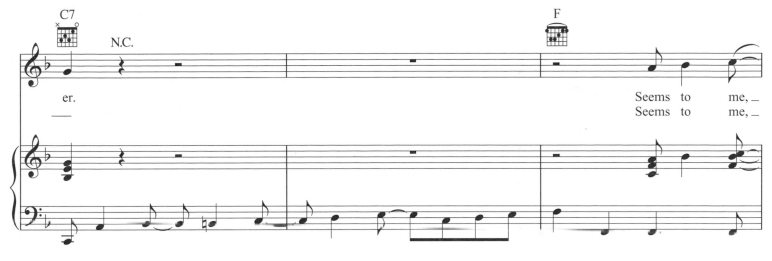

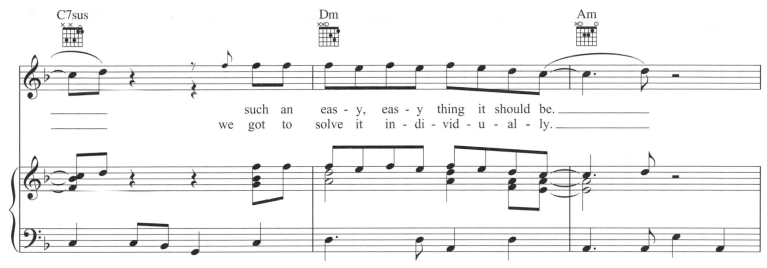

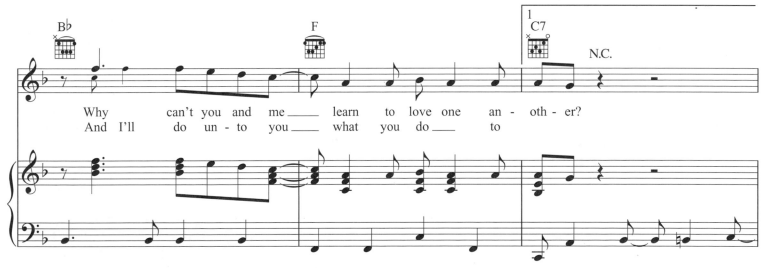

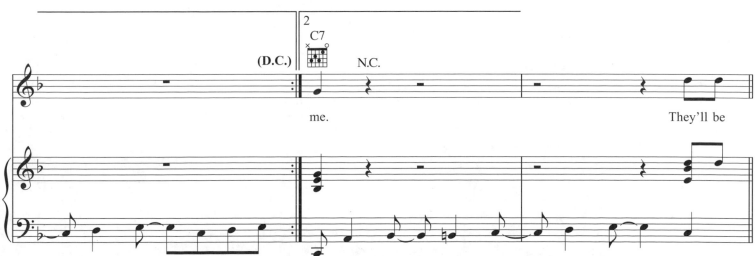

shout - in' from the moun - tain on out to the sea, _____
Oh, _____ what a feel - in' just come o - ver me. _____ It's e -

no two ways a - bout it, peo - ple have to be free. _____
nough to move a moun - tain, make a blind ____ man see. _____

Ask me my o - pin - ion, my o - pin - ion will be, _____ it's a
Ev - 'ry - bod - y's danc - in'; come on, let's ____ go see. _____ There's _

nat - 'ral sit - u - a - tion for a man to be free. _____
peace _ in the val - ley, now we all can be free. _____

PHILADELPHIA FREEDOM

Words and Music by ELTON JOHN
and BERNIE TAUPIN

I used to be a roll - ing stone, _
If you choose to, you can live your _

_ you know. _ If the cause _ was right, _ I'd leave _
_ life a - lone. _ Some peo - ple choose _ the cit - y, some oth -

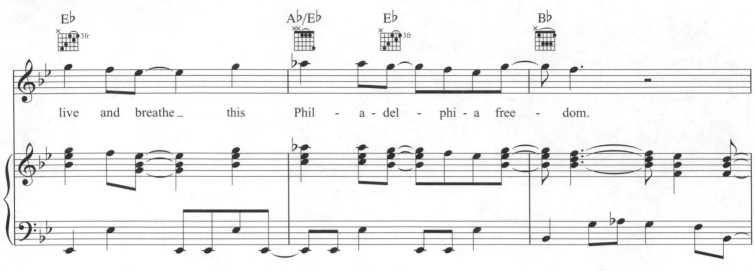

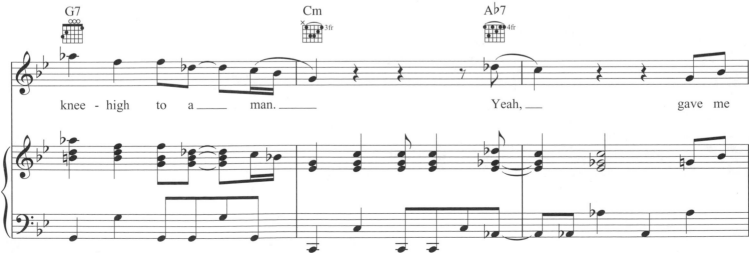

peace of mind __ my dad - dy nev - er had.

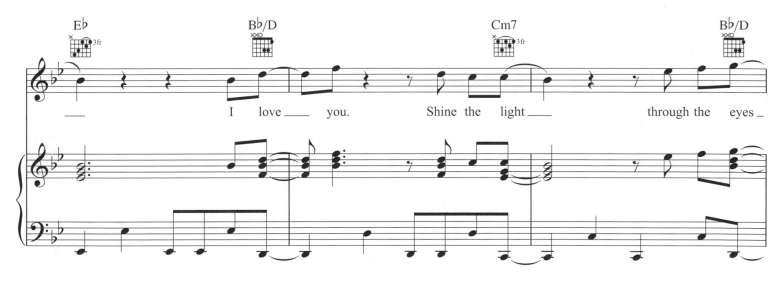

Oh, Phil - a - del - phi - a free - dom, __ shine on me. __

__ I love __ you. Shine the light __ through the eyes __

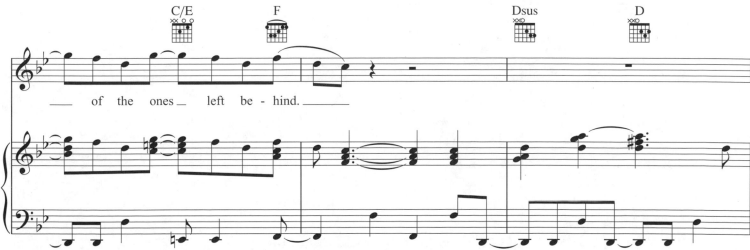

__ of the ones __ left be - hind. _____

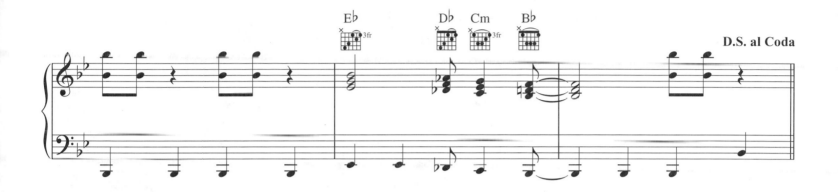

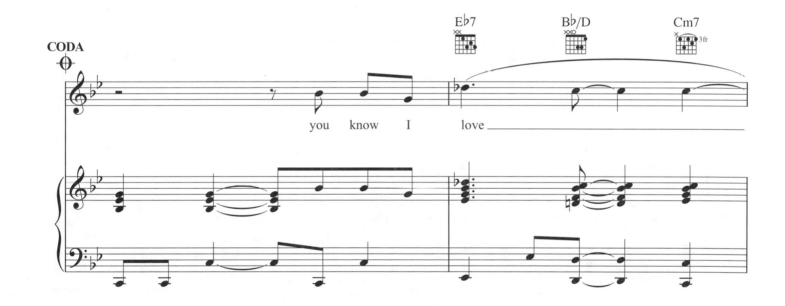

you know I love _____

_____ you,

you know I love _____

RAMBLIN' MAN

Words and Music by
DICKEY BETTS

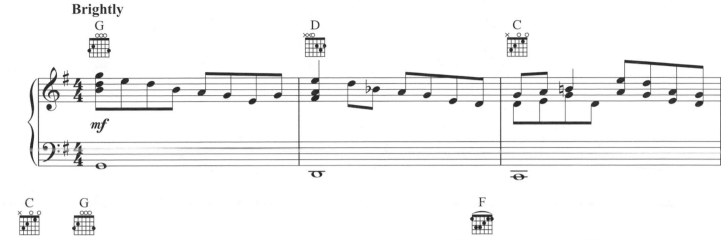

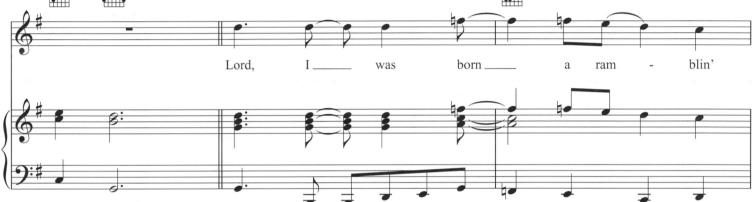

Lord, I ___ was born ___ a ram - blin'

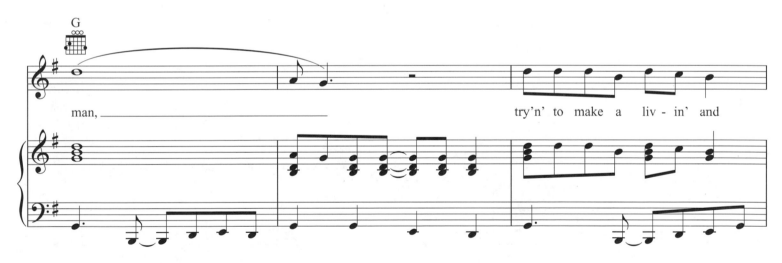

man, ___ try'n' to make a liv - in' and

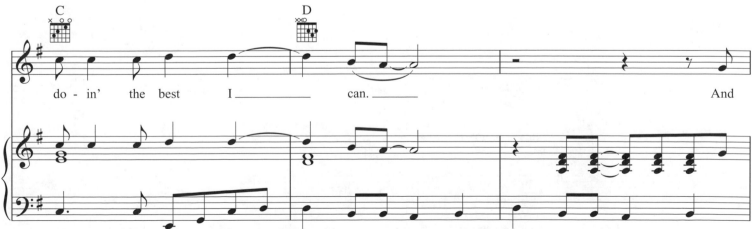

do - in' the best I ___ can. ___ And

when it's time ___ for leav - in', ___ I hope you'll un - der - stand ___

_____ that I was born ___ a ram - blin'

man. Well, my fa - ther was ___ a gam -
on my way ___ to New ___

- bler down in Geor - gia, ___ and he
___ Or - leans this morn - in', ___

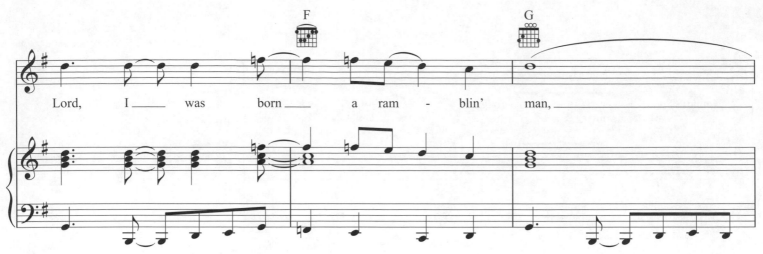

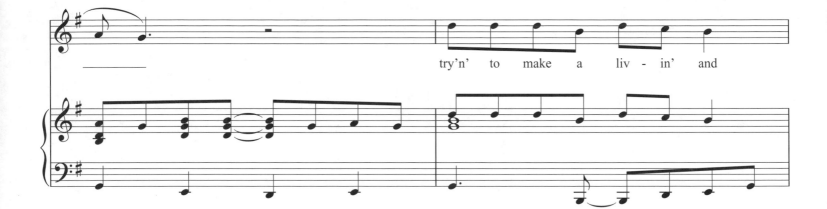

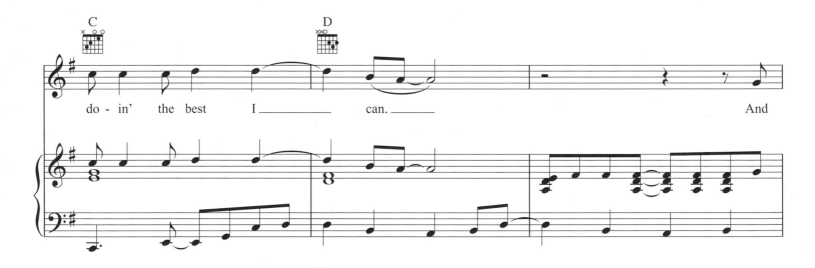

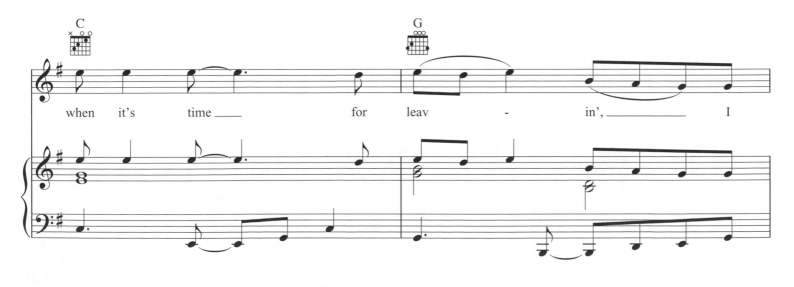

hope you'll un - der - stand _____ that I was born _

— a ram - blin' man. I'm

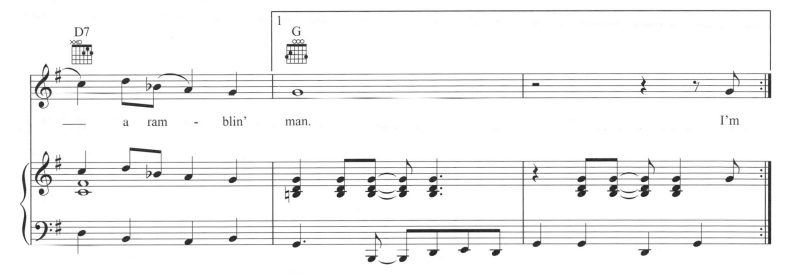

man. Lord, I ___ was born _

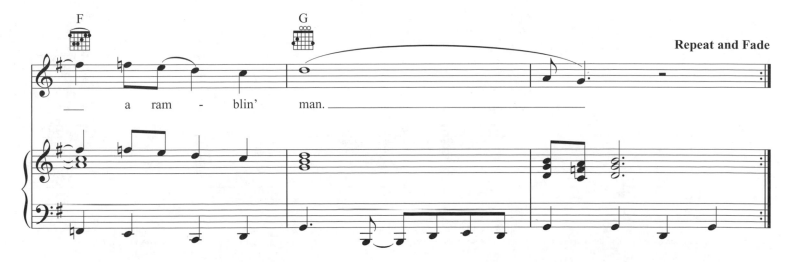

Repeat and Fade

— a ram - blin' man. _____

REDEMPTION SONG

Words and Music by
BOB MARLEY

112

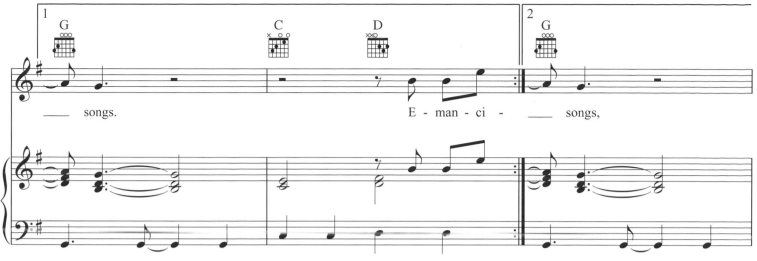

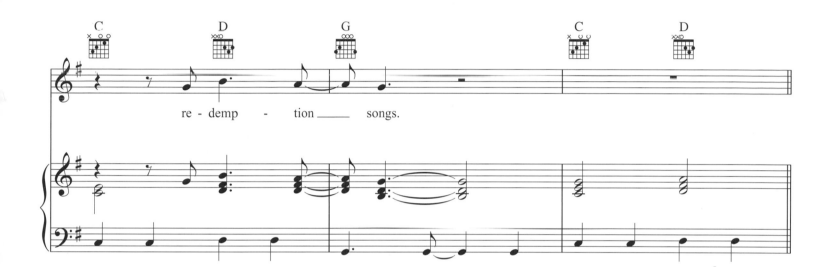

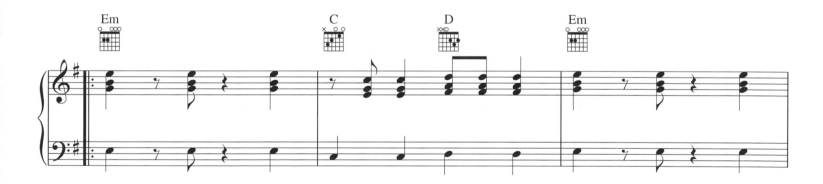

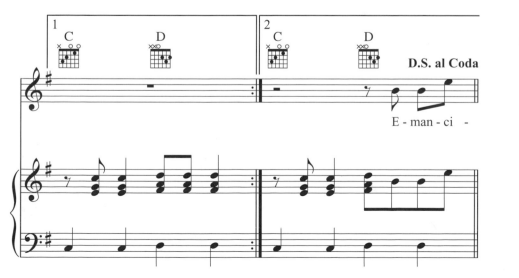

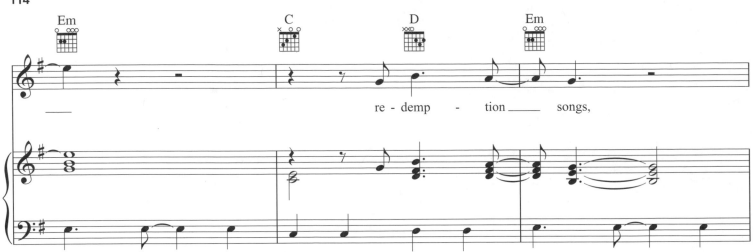

re - demp - tion ____ songs,

these ____ songs of free - dom, songs of free -

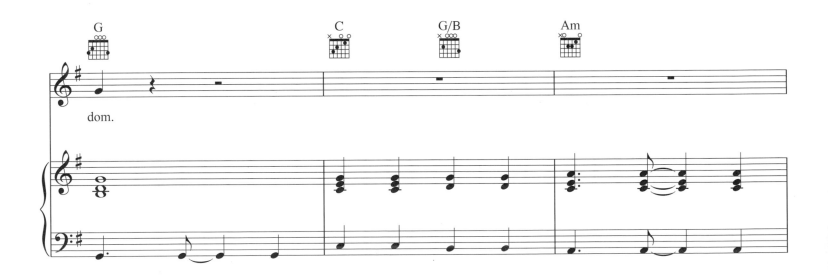

dom.

ROCKY MOUNTAIN HIGH

Words and Music by JOHN DENVER
and MIKE TAYLOR

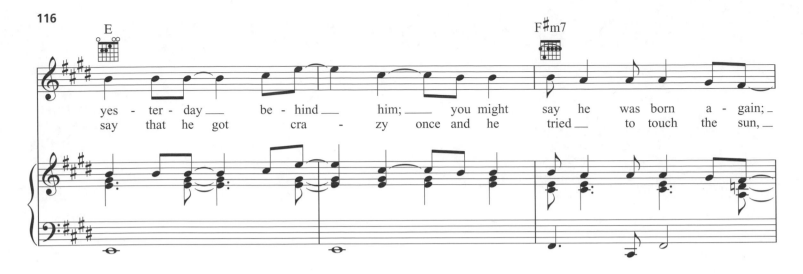

yes - ter - day ___ be - hind ___ him; ___ you might say he was born a - gain; ___
say that he got cra - zy once and he tried ___ to touch the sun, ___

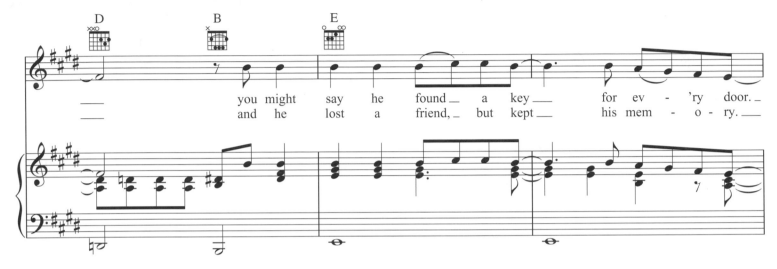

___ you might say he found ___ a key ___ for ev - 'ry door. ___
___ and he lost a friend, ___ but kept ___ his mem - o - ry. ___

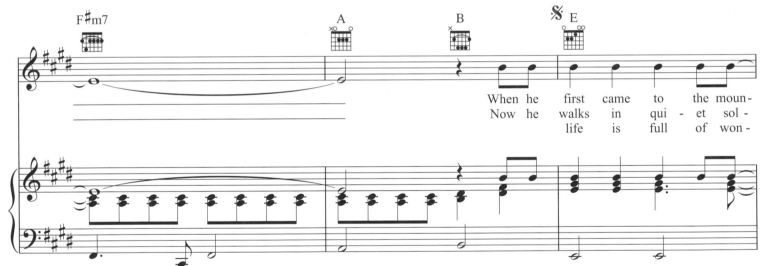

When he first came to the moun -
Now he walks in qui - et sol -
life is full of won -

- tains ___ his life ___ was far a - way, ___ on the road ___
- i - tude, the for - ests and the streams ___ seek - ing
- der, ___ but his heart ___ still knows some fear ___ of a

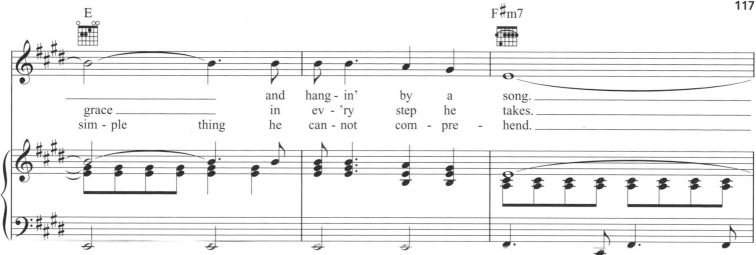

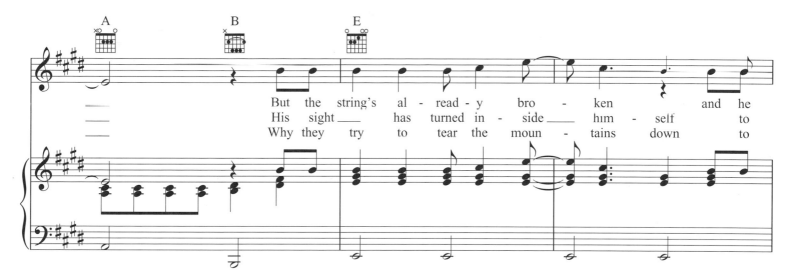

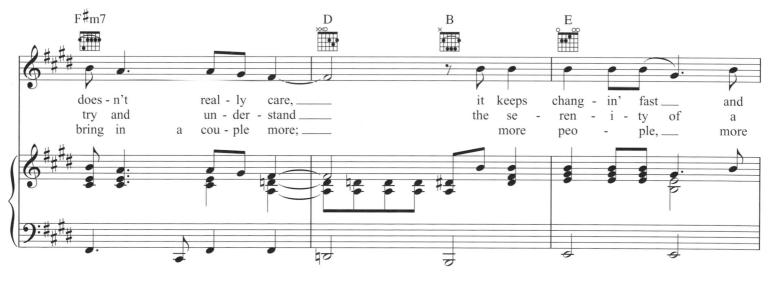

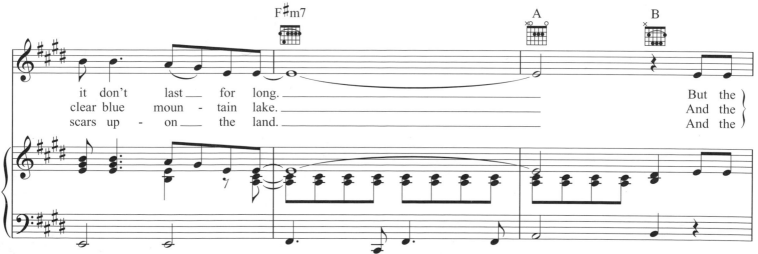

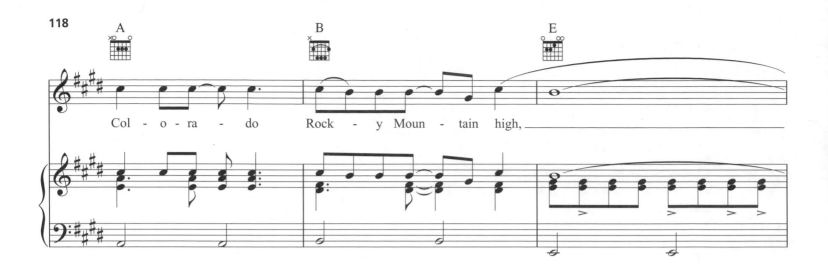

Col - o - ra - do Rock - y Moun - tain high, ____

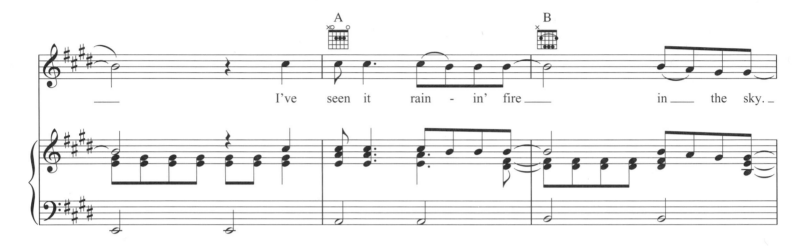

___ I've seen it rain - in' fire ___ in ___ the sky. __

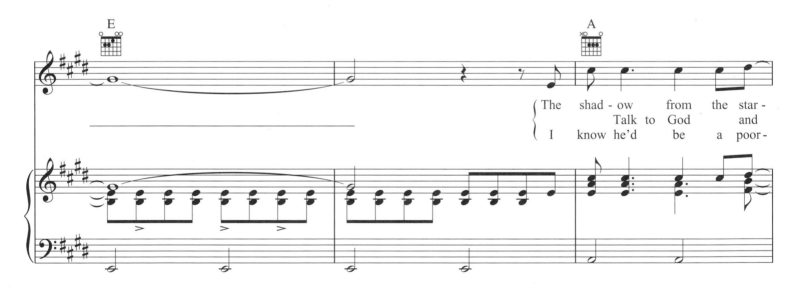

_____

The shad - ow from the star -
Talk to God and
I know he'd be a poor-

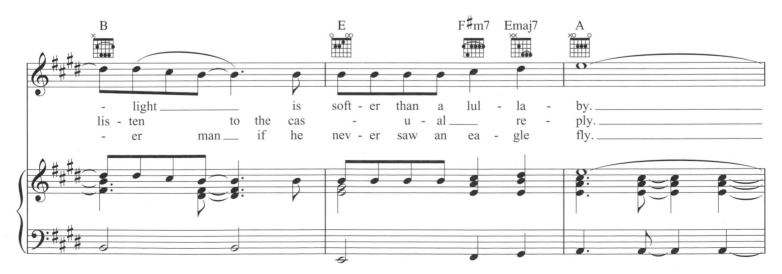

- light ____ is soft - er than a lul - la - by. ___
lis - ten to the cas - u - al re - ply. ___
- er man __ if he nev - er saw an ea - gle fly. ___

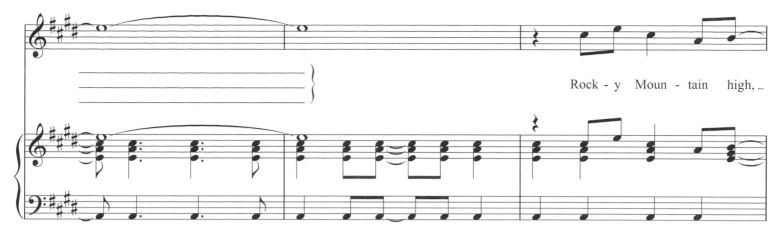

Rock - y Moun - tain high,

E   F#m7

Rock - y Moun - tain high.

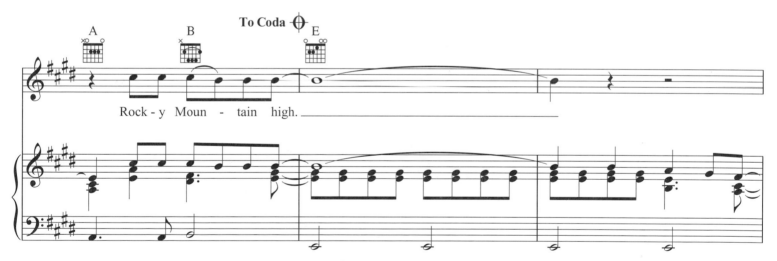

A   B   **To Coda** ⊕ E

Rock - y Moun - tain high. _____

F#m7

1
A   B

He climbed _

2
A   B   **D.S. al Coda**

Now his

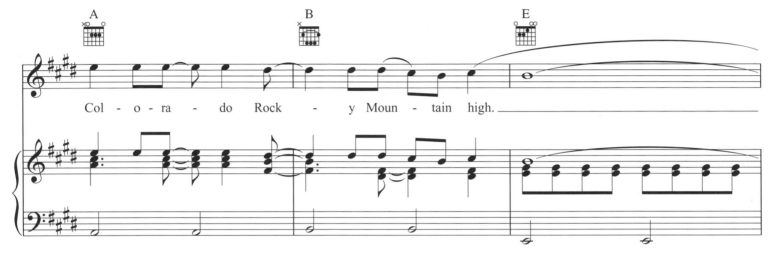

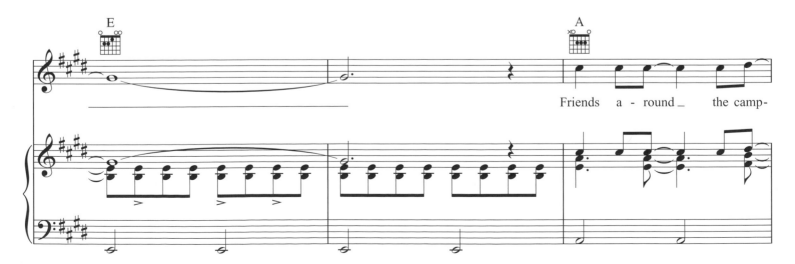

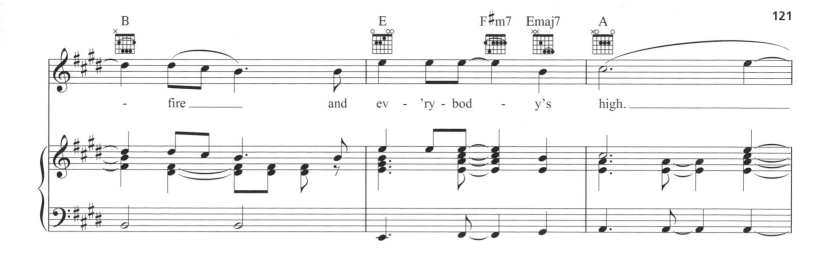

fire _____ and ev - 'ry - bod - y's high. _____

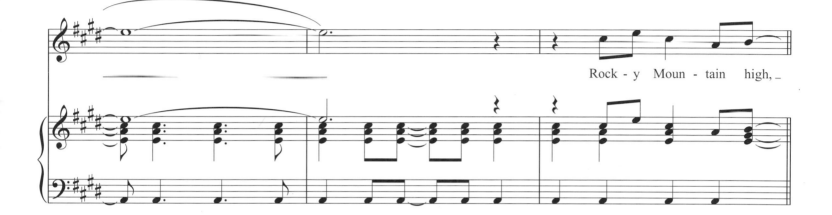

Rock - y Moun - tain high, _

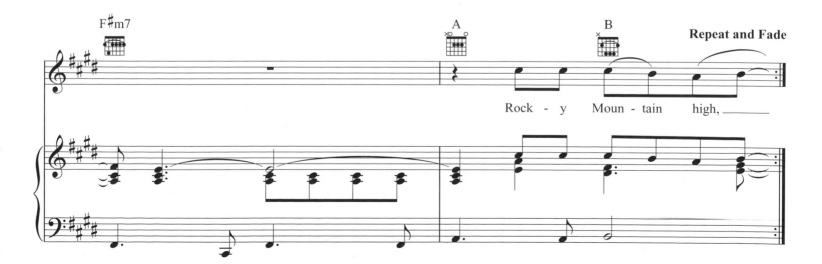

Rock - y Moun - tain high, _____

Repeat and Fade

SHARE THE LAND

Words and Music by
BURTON CUMMINGS

may-be I'll be there to share ___ the land ___ that they'll be giv-ing a - way ___ when we all live to-geth-

- er.

To Coda

Did you pay your dues,

did you read the news, this morn-ing when the pap-er land - ed ___ in your yard? ___

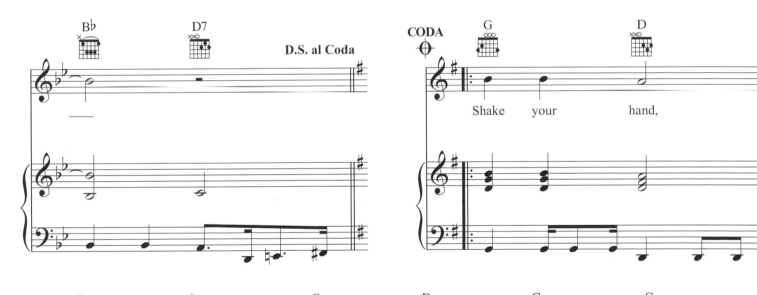

SIGNS

Words and Music by
LES EMMERSON

He said, "You look like a fine _ up-stand-ing young man, _ I think you'll _ do." _ So I

took off my hat, I said, "I-mag-ine that! _ Me work-ing for you!" _ Whoa. ____

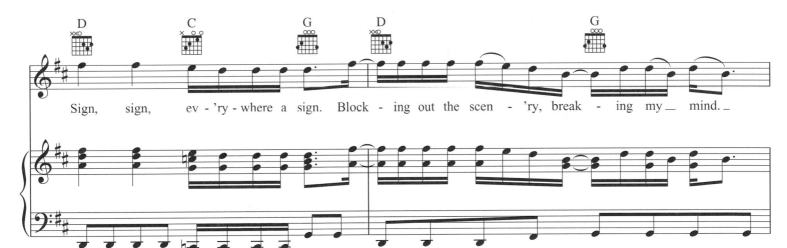

Sign, sign, ev-'ry-where a sign. Block-ing out the scen-'ry, break-ing my _ mind. _

Do this, don't _ do _ that. _ Can't you read ____ the sign? ____

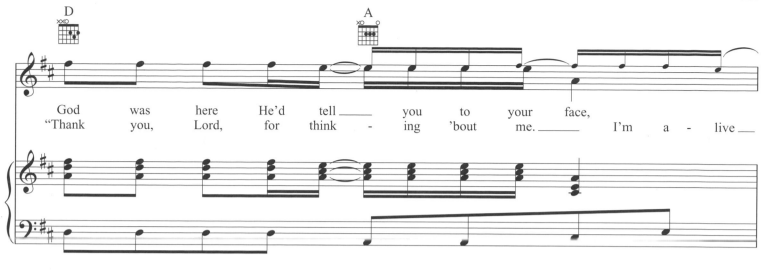

God was here He'd tell _____ you to your face,

"Thank you, Lord, for think - ing 'bout me. _____ I'm a - live _____

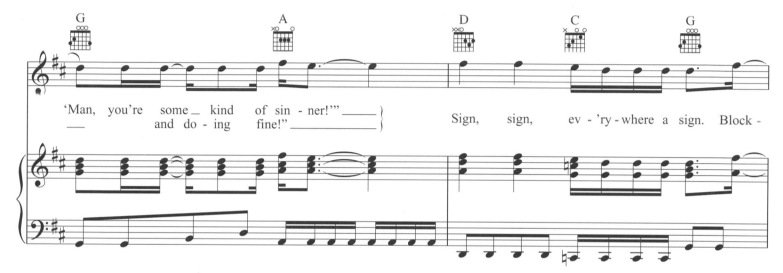

'Man, you're some _ kind of sin - ner!'" _____ }
_____ and do - ing fine!" _____ }

Sign, sign, ev - 'ry - where a sign. Block -

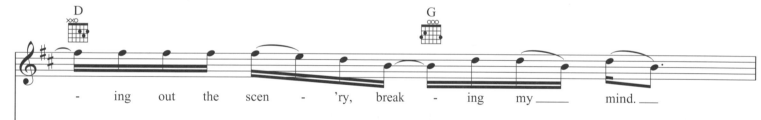

- ing out the scen - 'ry, break - ing my _____ mind. _____

Do this, don't _ do _ that. _ Can't you read _____ the sign? _____

To Coda

Now, hey you, mis - ter, can't_ you read? ____ You've

got to have a shirt and tie _____ to get a seat. _____ You

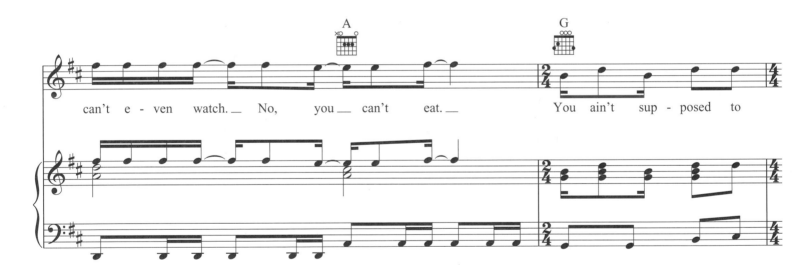

can't e - ven watch._ No, you_ can't eat._ You ain't sup - posed to

be here. _____

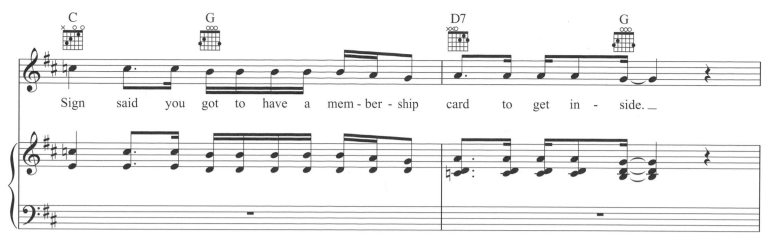

Sign said you got to have a mem - ber - ship card to get in - side. __

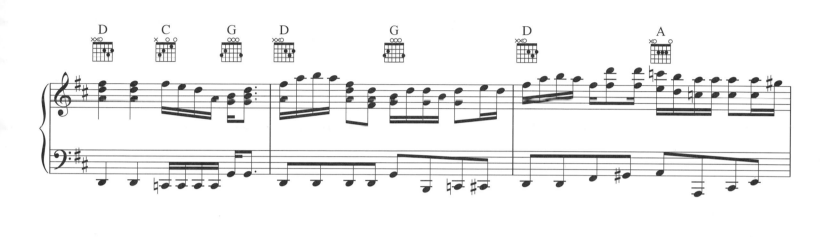

And the

Sign, sign, ev - 'ry - where a sign.

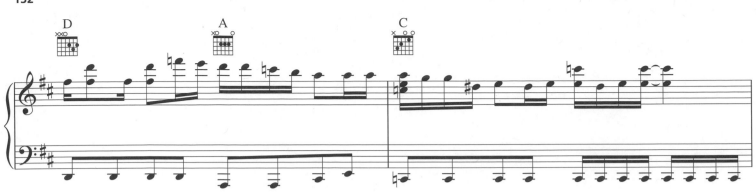

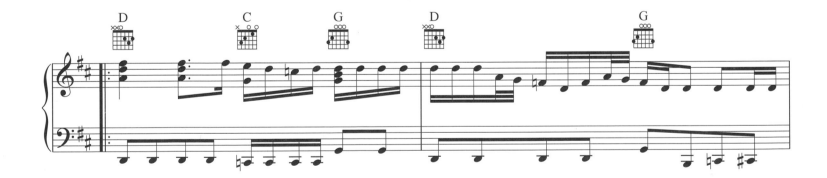

Repeat and Fade

Optional Ending

(Sittin' On)
THE DOCK OF THE BAY

Words and Music by STEVE CROPPER
and OTIS REDDING

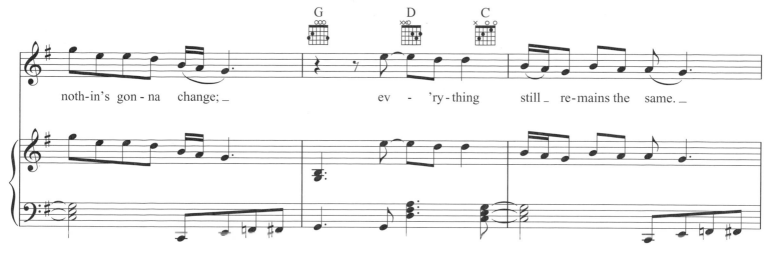

noth-in's gon - na change; __ ev - 'ry-thing still __ re-mains the same. __

I can't do what ten peo-ple tell me __ to do, __ so I guess I'll re-main __

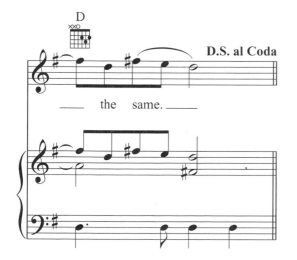

__ the same. __

D.S. al Coda

CODA

Repeat and Fade

Optional Ending

SIMPLE SONG OF FREEDOM

Words and Music by
BOBBY DARIN

Come and sing a sim - ple song___ of free -

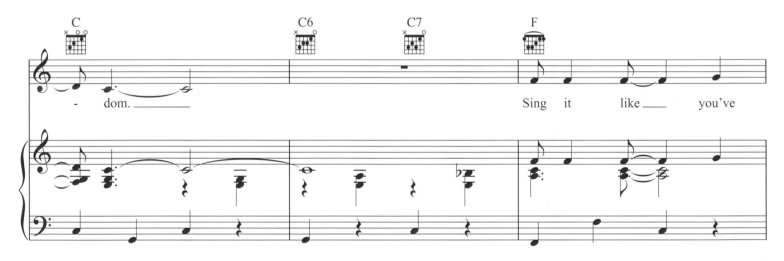

- dom._____ Sing it like___ you've

nev - er sung be - fore.____

Let it fill the air,____ tell the peo - ple ev - 'ry - where _

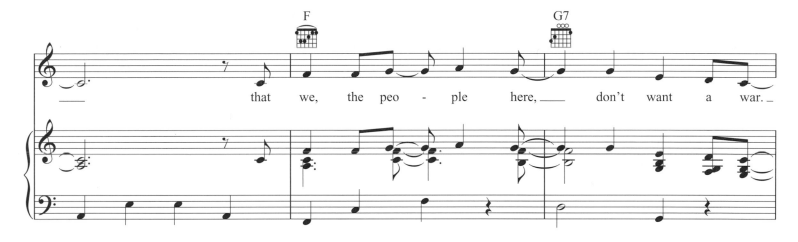

____ that we, the peo - ple here, ____ don't want a war. _

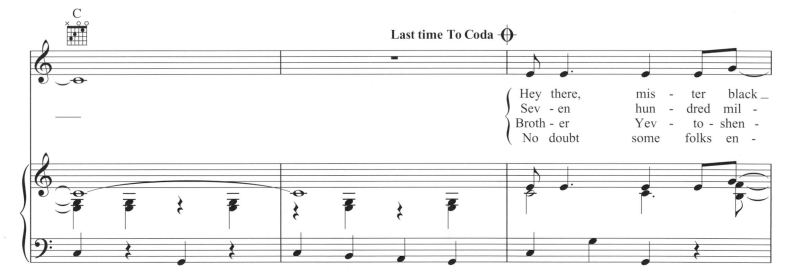

Last time To Coda

Hey there, mis - ter black _
Sev - en hun - dred mil -
Broth - er Yev - to - shen -
No doubt some folks en -

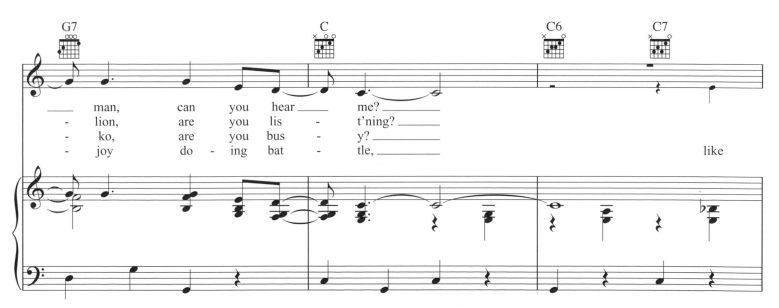

____ man, can you hear ____ me? ____
- lion, are you lis - t'ning? ____
- ko, are you bus - y? ____
- joy do - ing bat - tle, ____ like

I don't want your dia - monds or your game. ____
Most of what you read ____ is made of lies. ____
If not, won't you drop ____ a friend a line ____
pres - i - dents, prime min - is - ters and kings. ____

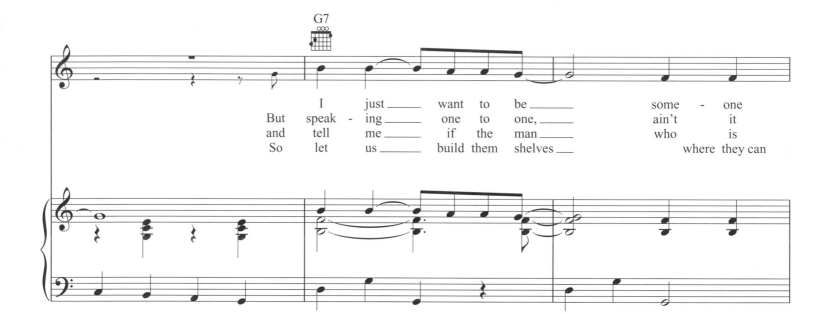

I just ____ want to be ____ some - one
But speak - ing ____ one to one, ____ ain't it
and tell me ____ if the man ____ who is
So let us ____ build them shelves ____ where they can

known to you as me ____ and I will bet ____ my life ____
ev - 'ry - bod - y's sun ____ to wake up in ____ the morn -
plow - ing up your land ____ has got the war ____ ma - chine __
fight a - mong them - selves ____ and leave the peo - ple be ____

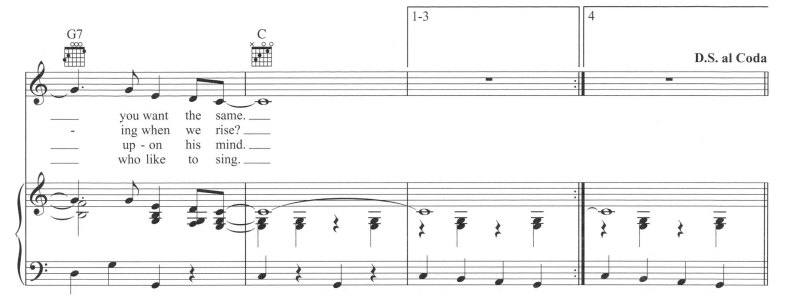

you want the same.
-ing when we rise?
up-on his mind.
who like to sing.

Let it fill the air, _____ tell the peo-

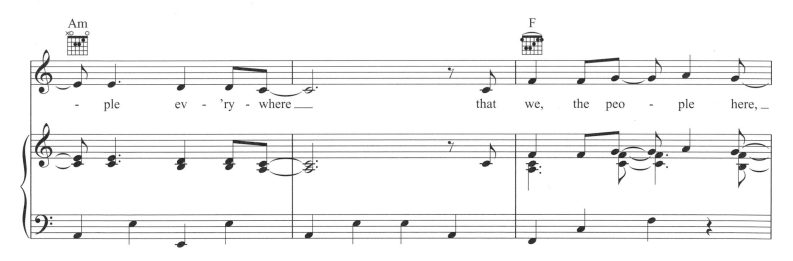

-ple ev-'ry-where _____ that we, the peo-ple here, _

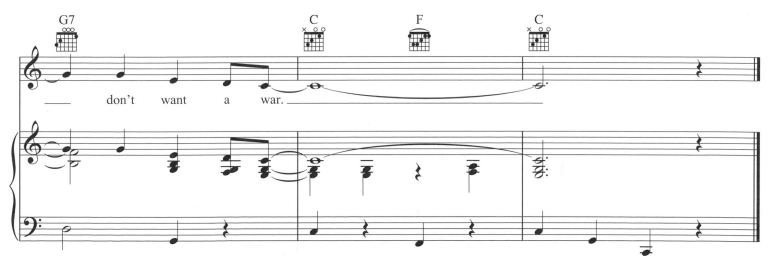

_____ don't want a war. _____

SOMEBODY TO LOVE

Words and Music by
DARBY SLICK

With a steady beat

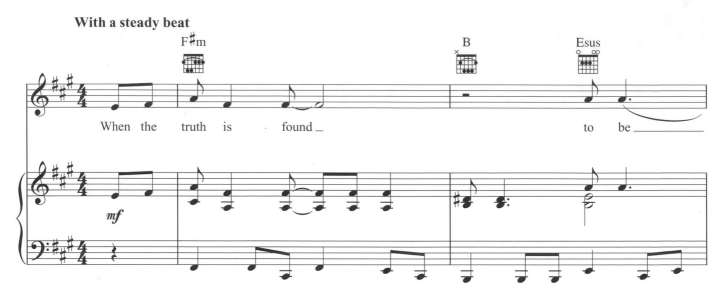

When the truth is found ___ to be ___

___ lies, and all ___ the joy ___

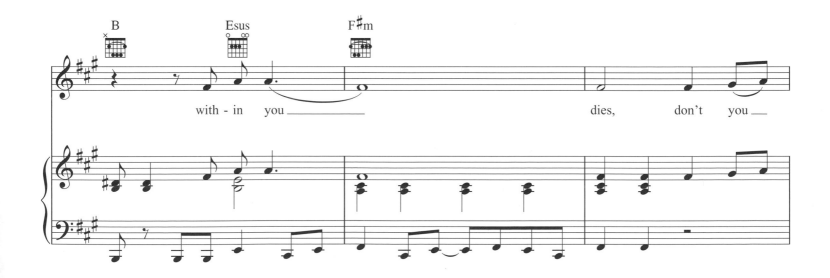

with - in you ___ dies, don't you ___

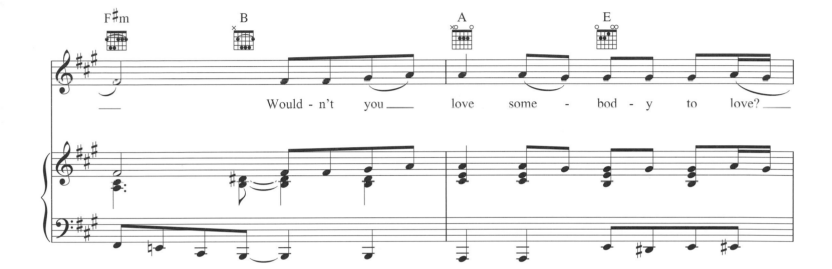

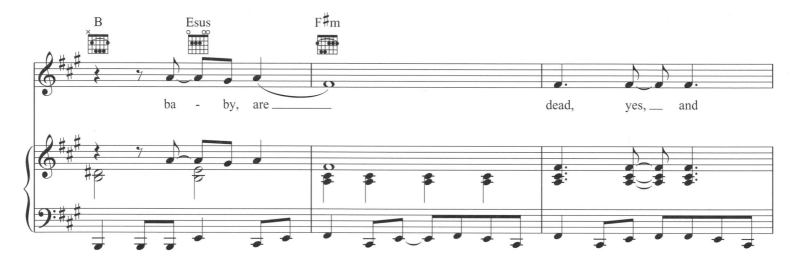

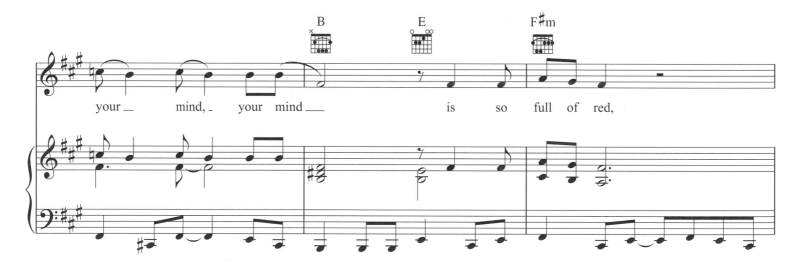

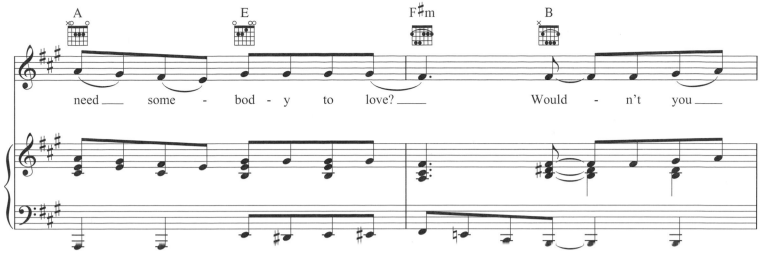

need ___ some - bod - y to love? ___ Would - n't you ___

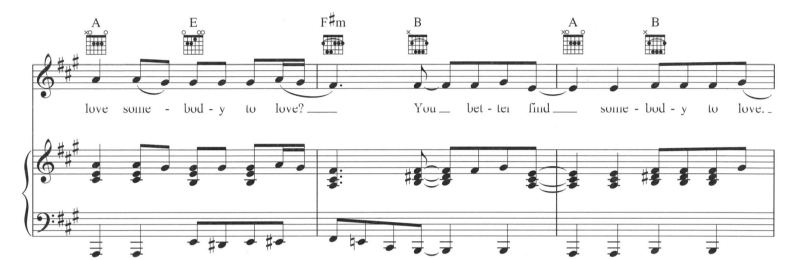

love some - bod - y to love? ___ You ___ bet - ter find ___ some - bod - y to love. ___

___ Your eyes, ___ I say your eyes ___ may

look like his. ___ Yeah, but in your head, ba - by, ___

144

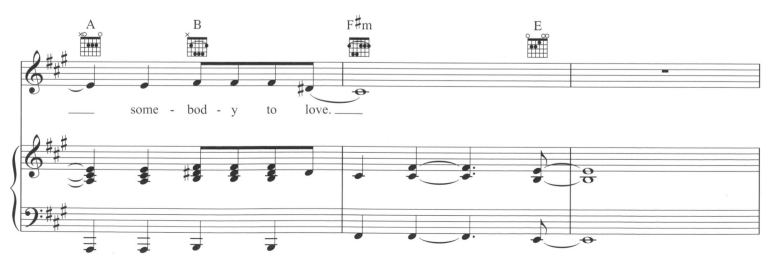

Tears_ are run - ning, _____ they're_ all run -

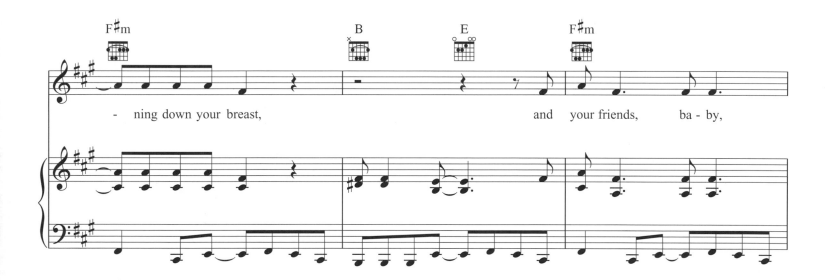

- ning down your breast, and your friends, ba - by,

they treat you like_ a guest. _____ Don't you _

want some-bod-y to love? ___ Don't _ you need some-bod-y to love? _

___ Would-n't you ___ love some-bod-y to love? ___ You bet-ter find _

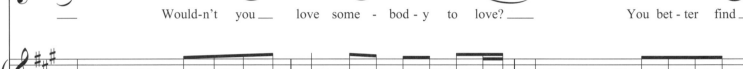

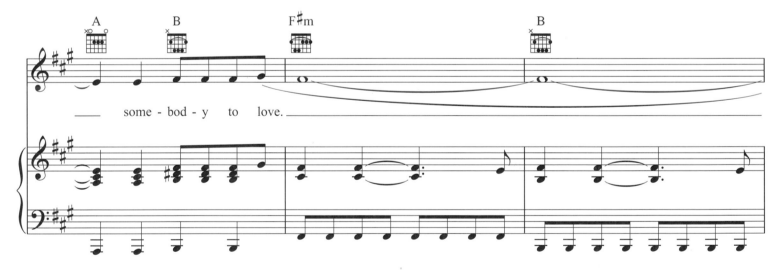

___ some-bod-y to love. _____

SUNSHINE
(Go Away Today)

Written by
JONATHAN EDWARDS

I'll buy __ it. The time is all __ we've _ lost. ___ I'll try __ it, 'n'

he can't e - ven run _____ his own _ life; _ I'll be damned if he'll _ run mine! _

Sun - shine, _ Sun - shine, _

D.S. al Coda

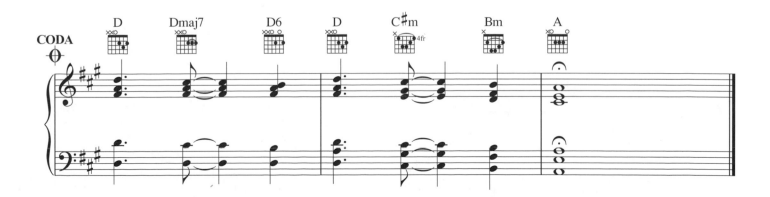

THIS LAND IS YOUR LAND

Words and Music by
WOODY GUTHRIE

Bright and cheerful

As I went

(1.) walk - ing that rib - bon of high - way I saw a -
(2.,4.,6.) your land, this land is my land, from Cal - i -
(3.) ram - bled and I fol - lowed my foot - steps to the spar - kling
(5.) shin - ing, and I was stroll - ing; the wheat fields

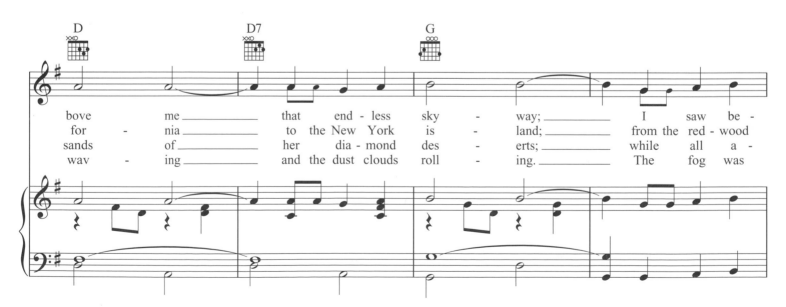

bove me that end - less sky - way; I saw be -
for - nia to the New York is - land; from the red - wood
sands of her dia - mond des - erts; while all a -
wav - ing and the dust clouds roll - ing. The fog was

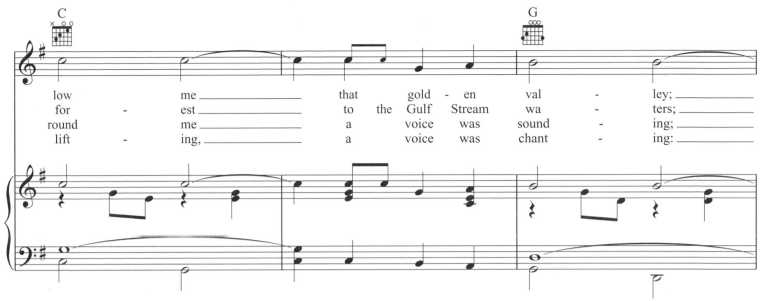

low me _____ that gold - en val - ley; _____
for - est _____ to the Gulf Stream wa - ters; _____
round me _____ a voice was sound - ing; _____
lift - ing, _____ a voice was chant - ing: _____

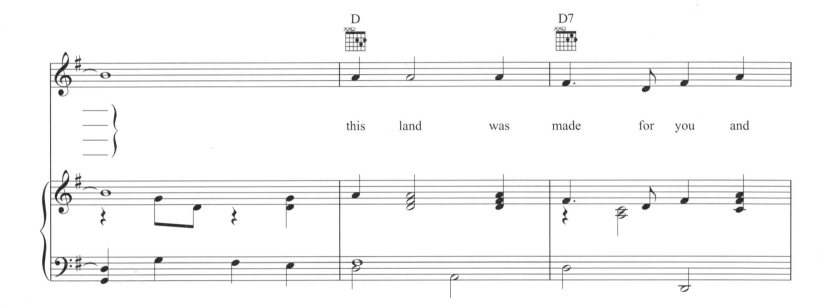

this land was made for you and

me. _____

(2., 4., 6. This land is
 3. I've roamed and
 5. Well, the sun came

me. _____

rit.

THREE LITTLE BIRDS

Words and Music by
BOB MARLEY

Moderately slow Reggae

"Don't wor - ry a - bout _ a thing, _ 'cause

ev - 'ry lit - tle thing gon - na be al - right." _ Sing - in', "Don't

wor - ry a - bout _ a thing, _ 'cause

ev - 'ry lit - tle thing gon - na be al - right." _ Rise up this

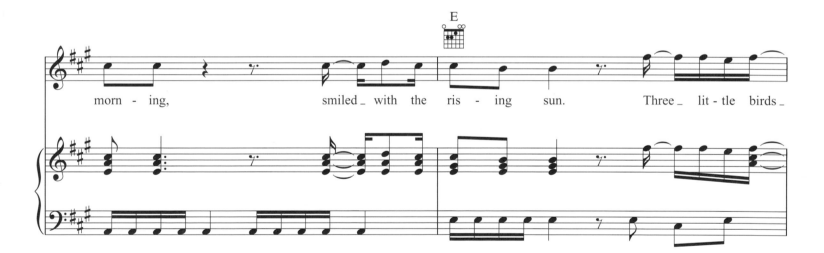

morn - ing, smiled _ with the ris - ing sun. Three _ lit - tle birds _

_ pitch by my door - step, sing - in' sweet _

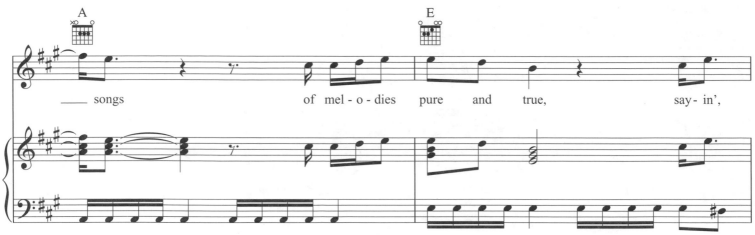

___ songs of mel - o - dies pure and true, say - in',

"This is my mes-sage to you - u - u." Sing-in', "Don't u - u." Sing-in', "Don't

wor - ry a - bout __ a thing, __ 'cause

Repeat and Fade

ev - 'ry lit - tle thing gon - na be al - right." __ Sing-in', "Don't

THE TIMES THEY ARE A-CHANGIN'

Words and Music by
BOB DYLAN

soon you'll be drenched to the bone, _____ if your

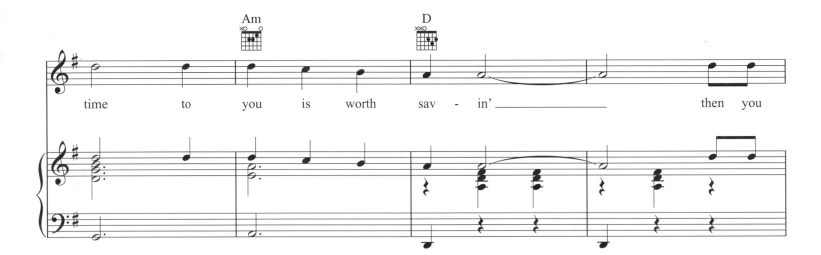

time to you is worth sav - in' _____ then you

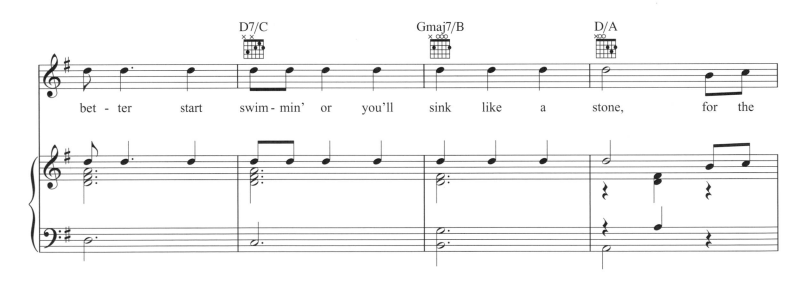

bet - ter start swim - min' or you'll sink like a stone, for the

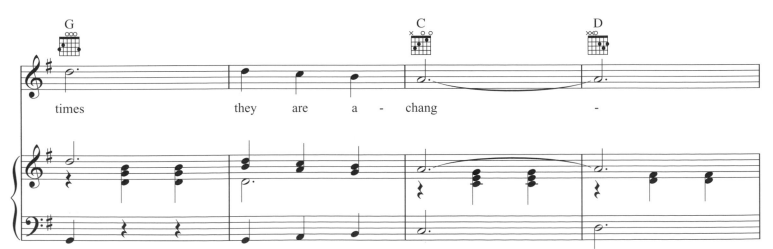

times they are a - chang -

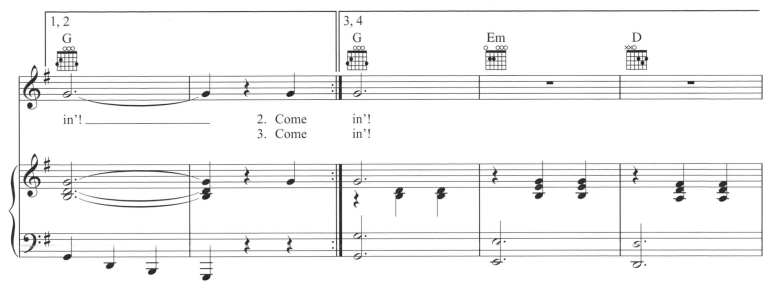

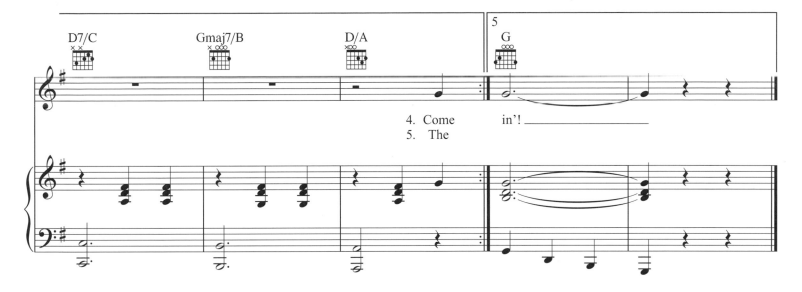

Additional Lyrics

2. Come writers and critics
Who prophesy with your pen
And keep your eyes wide
The chance won't come again.
And don't speak too soon
For the wheel's still in spin,
And there's no tellin' who
That it's namin'.
For the loser now
Will be later to win
For the times they are a-changin'!

3. Come senators, congressmen
Please heed the call
Don't stand in the doorway
Don't block up the hall.
For he that gets hurt
Will be he who has stalled,
There's a battle
Outside and it's ragin'.
It'll soon shake your windows
And rattle your walls
For the times they are a-changin'!

4. Come mothers and fathers
Throughout the land
And don't criticize
What you can't understand.
Your sons and your daughters
Are beyond your command,
Your old road is
Rapidly agin'.
Please get out of the new one
If you can't lend your hand
For the times they are a-changin'!

5. The line it is drawn
The curse it is cast
The slow one now will
Later be fast.
As the present now
Will later be past,
The order is rapidly fadin'.
And the first one now
Will later be last
For the times they are a-changin'!

WE MAY NEVER PASS THIS WAY AGAIN

Words and Music by JAMES SEALS
and DASH CROFTS

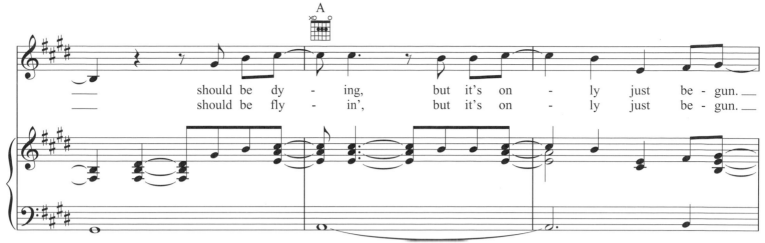

should be dy - ing, but it's on - ly just be - gun.
should be fly - in', but it's on - ly just be - gun.

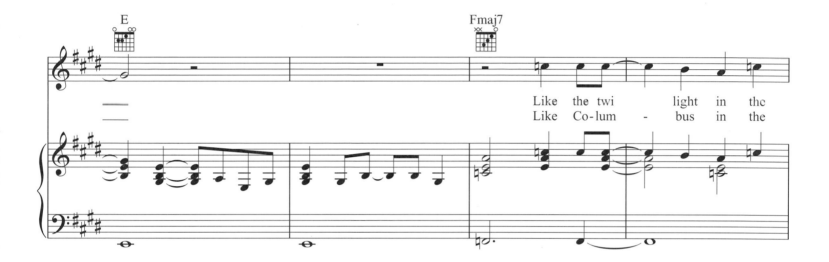

Like the twi - light in the
Like Co - lum - bus in the

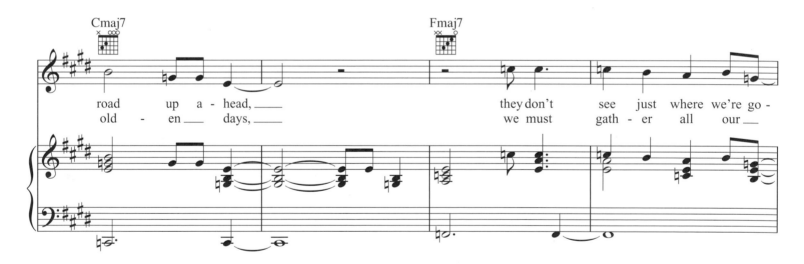

road up a - head, they don't see just where we're go -
old - en days, we must gath - er all our

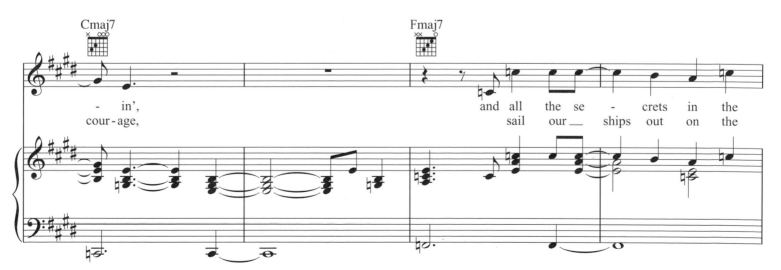

- in', and all the se - crets in the
cour - age, sail our ships out on the

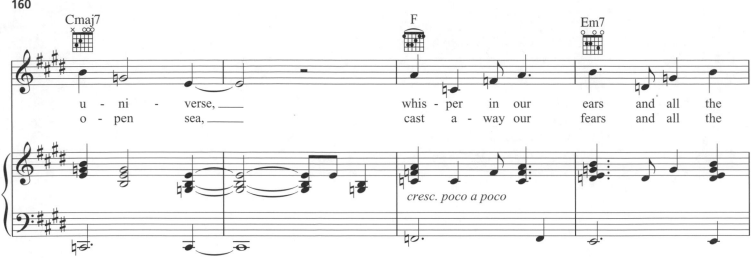

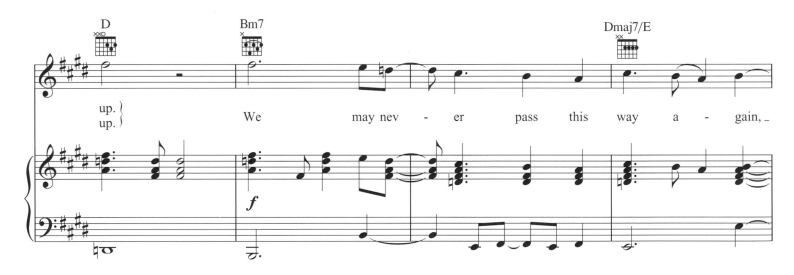

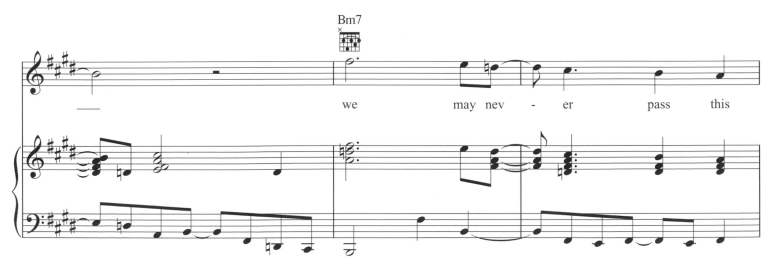

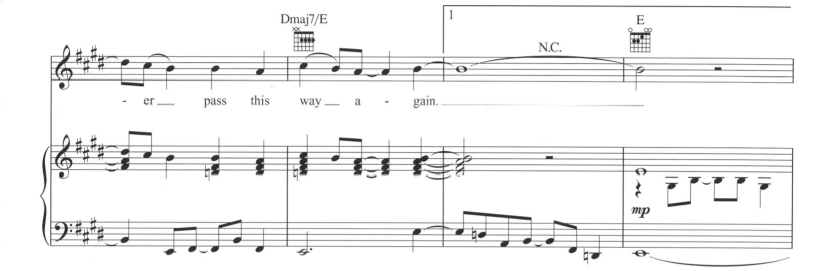

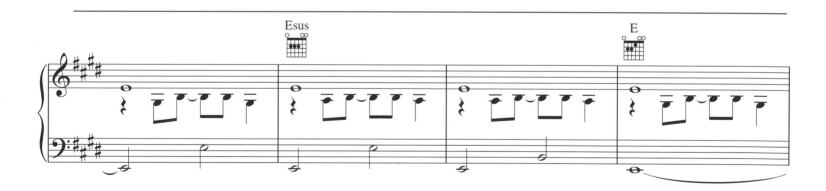

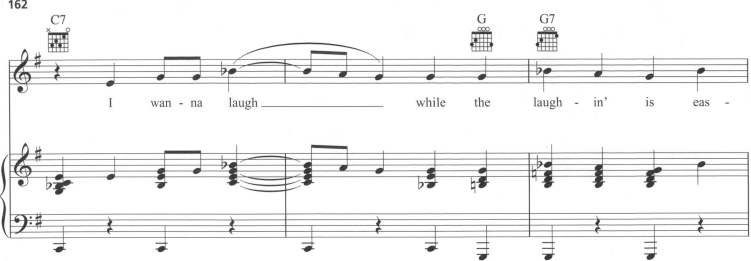

ba - by.

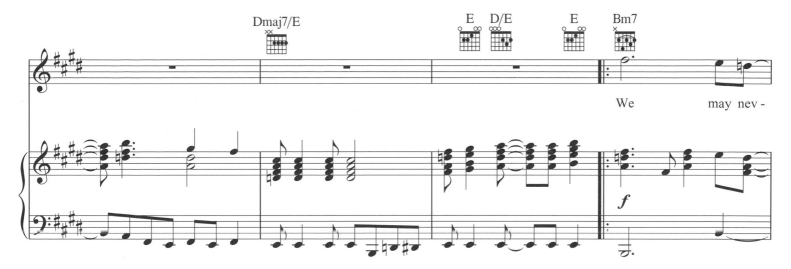

We may nev-

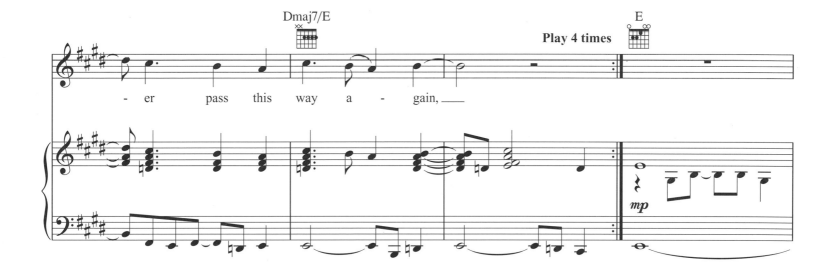

-er pass this way a - gain, __

Play 4 times

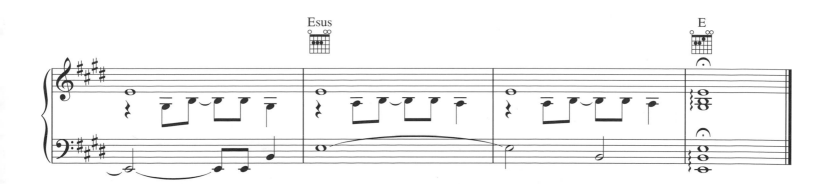

WE SHALL OVERCOME

Words based on 1901 hymn by
C. Albert Findley entitled "I'll Overcome Some Day"
Music based on 1794 hymn entitled "O Sanctissima"

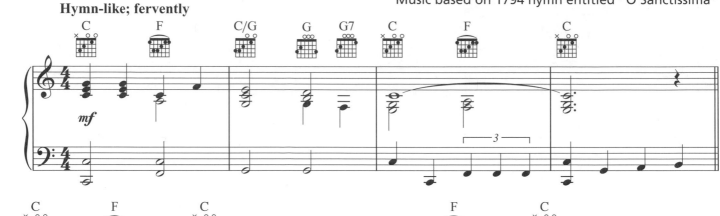

We shall o- ver - come. ___ We shall o- ver - come. ___
We shall live in peace. ___ We shall live in peace. ___

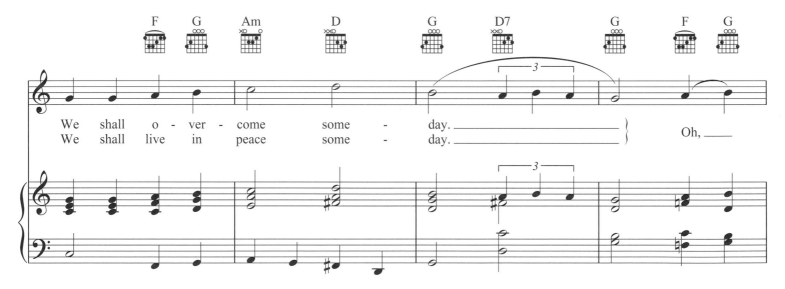

We shall o- ver - come some - day. ___ Oh, ___
We shall live in peace some - day. ___

deep in my heart I do be - lieve.

We shall o - ver - come some - day.
We'll walk hand in hand. ____
We are not a - fraid. ____

We'll walk hand in hand. ____
We are not a - fraid. ____
We'll walk hand in hand some - day. ____
We are not a - fraid to - day. ____

Oh, ____ deep in my heart I do be - lieve.

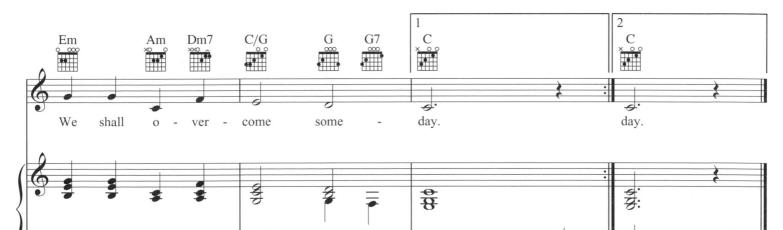

We shall o - ver - come some - day.
day.

WHAT'S GOING ON

Words and Music by RENALDO BENSON,
ALFRED CLEVELAND and MARVIN GAYE

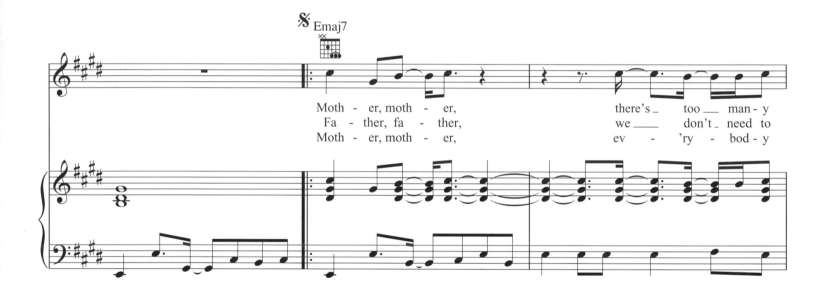

Moth- er, moth- er, there's_ too __ man - y
Fa - ther, fa - ther, we ____ don't_ need to
Moth- er, moth- er, ev - 'ry - bod- y

of you cry - ing.
es - ca - late. ____
thinks we're wrong. ____

Broth- er, broth- er, broth - er,
You see, _ war is not __ the an - swer,
Ah, but _ who are they_ to judge_ us

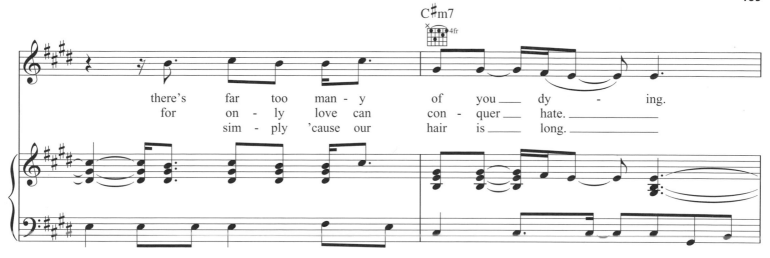

there's far too man-y of you____ dy - ing.
for on - ly love can con - quer____ hate._____
sim - ply 'cause our hair is____ long._____

You ___ know ___ we've got to find ___ a way ___ to bring some
You ___ know ___ we've got to find ___ a way ___ to bring some
Ah, you know ___ we've got to find ___ a way ___ to bring some un - der -

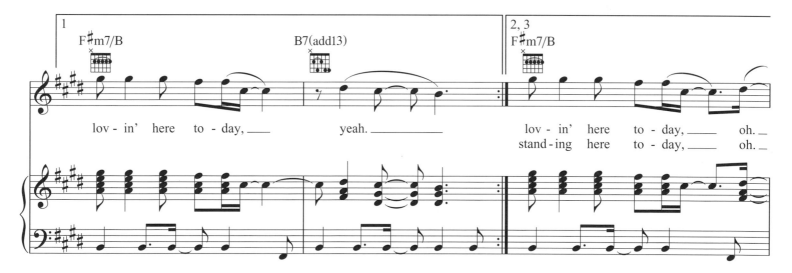

| 1 | | 2, 3 |

F#m7/B ... B7(add13) ... F#m7/B

lov - in' here to - day, ____ yeah._____ lov - in' here to - day, ____ oh.___
standing here to - day, ____ oh.___

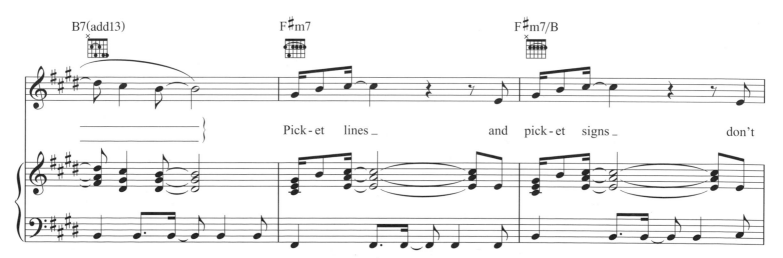

B7(add13) ... F#m7 ... F#m7/B

_____ Pick - et lines ___ and pick - et signs ___ don't

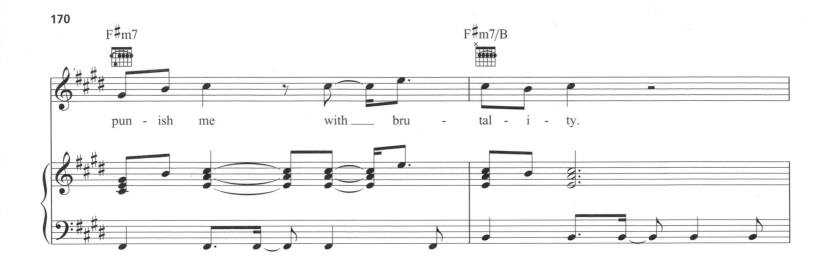

Be, doot, de ___ doot; Be, ___ be, be, ___ doot; Be ___ be, be, ___ doot;

D.S. al Coda
(take 2nd ending)

Bu, doot, be, ___ be, be, ___ doot; Be ___ be, be, ___ be, be, ___ doot.

CODA

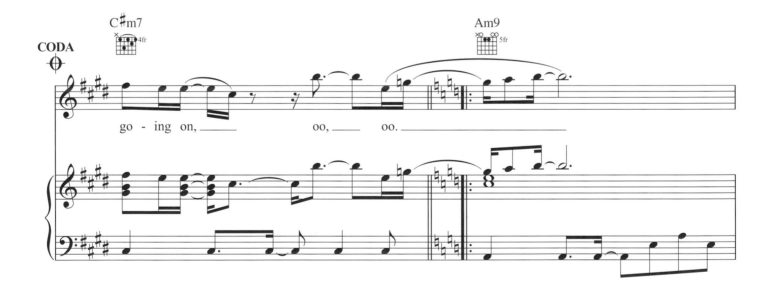

go - ing on, ___ oo, ___ oo. ___

I, ___ yi, yi, yi, ___ yi, yi, ___ yi, ya, ___

ya, ya, ___ ya.

I, ___ yi, yi, ___ yi, yi, ___ yi, ya, ___ ya, yu, ___ ya, ya. ___

A/B

Be, doot, de, ___ doot; Be, ___ be, be, ___ doot; Be ___ be, be, ___ doot;

Repeat and Fade

Bu, doot, be, ___ be, be, ___ doot; Be, ___ be, be, ___ be, be, ___ doot. Oo. ___

WAR

Words and Music by NORMAN WHITFIELD
and BARRETT STRONG

War means tears ___ in thou - sands of moth-ers' eyes ___ when their

Fade on last repeat

sons go out to fight ___ and lose ___ their ___ lives. ___ I said:

Additional Lyrics

2. War, uh! What is it good for? Absolutely nothing; say it again;
   War, uh! What is it good for? Absolutely nothing.
   War, it ain't nothing but a heartbreaker;
   War, friend only to the undertaker.
   War is an enemy to all mankind.
   The thought of war blows my mind.
   War has caused unrest within the younger generation;
   Induction then destruction, who wants to die? Ah

3. War, uh um; What is it good for? You tell me nothing, um!
   War, uh! What is it good for? Absolutely nothing.
   Good God, war, it's nothing but a heartbreaker;
   War, friend only to the undertaker.
   Wars have shattered many a young man's dreams;
   Made him disabled, bitter and mean.
   Life is much too short and precious to spend fighting wars each day.
   War can't give life, it can only take it away. Ah

4. War, Uh um! What is it good for? Absolutely nothing, um.
   War, good God almighty, listen, what is it good for? Absolutely nothing, yeah.
   War, it ain't nothing but a heartbreaker;
   War, friend only to the undertaker.
   Peace, love and understanding,
   Tell me is there no place for them today?
   They say we must fight to keep our freedom,
   But Lord knows it's gotta be a better way.

5. I say war, uh um, yeah, yeah. What is it good for? Absolutely nothing; say it again;
   War, yea, yea, yea, yea, what is it good for? Absolutely nothing; say it again;
   War, nothing but a heartbreaker; What is it good for? Friend only to the undertaker....
   (Fade)